George Makepeace Towle

Magellan

The first voyage round the world

George Makepeace Towle

Magellan
The first voyage round the world

ISBN/EAN: 9783744723015

Printed in Europe, USA, Canada, Australia, Japan

Cover: Foto ©Andreas Hilbeck / pixelio.de

More available books at **www.hansebooks.com**

MAGELLAN

First Around the World

BY

GEORGE M. TOWLE

ILLUSTRATED

BOSTON
LOTHROP, LEE & SHEPARD CO.

PREFACE.

MAGELLAN performed a voyage far more difficult, perilous, and uncertain than that of Vasco da Gama; and as an explorer of the ocean, he was not less persistent and dauntless. As Vasco found the water-way to Asia around the Cape of Good Hope, so Magellan, a little more than twenty years after, discovered the route to the same mysterious continent, by sailing westward instead of eastward, and by passing through the stormy straits, at the extreme southern point of the South American Continent, which still perpetuate his name and renown.

He crossed not only the Atlantic, but the Pacific also, and bestowed its gentle name upon the latter ocean; and one of his ships was the first to sail completely around the globe, though Magellan did not himself live to assist in achieving this great triumph of navigation.

Besides encountering the many perils of the sea, the harrowing hardships of famine, the terrible scourges of disease, and threatened destruction by conspiracy and revolt, it was Magellan's fate to engage in fierce conflicts with savage tribes, and to meet with treachery at their hands, as well as to receive from them honest welcome and bounteous hospitality. No voyage, indeed, could be imagined, into which every feature of romance and adventure, of narrow escape and brilliant achievement, could be more crowded, than was that of Magellan from the port of Cadiz to the island clusters of Australasia.

Magellan's own character is well fitted to call forth the young reader's admiration. It was his ambition, not to enter upon a career of blood-shed and conquest, nor, mainly, to acquire wealth, honors, or power for himself; but to achieve for the civilized world the vast benefits which he knew would follow the discovery of a route around the American Continent, and to confer upon heathen barbarians the blessings of what he devoutly believed to be the true faith.

He was generous and noble in disposition; never wantonly cruel; indulgent to and beloved by those whom he commanded; brave as a lion, and indomitable in perseverance and tenacity of purpose; undismayed by any obstacle, however formidable; and reso-

/ute in subduing men and circumstances to the end he
had in view ; easily angered, but brief in his anger ;
humane, considerate, and large-hearted.

The story of his famous expedition comprises one
of the most important as well as thrilling portions of
the world's history ; and can scarcely fail to interest
as well as inform those who peruse it.

CONTENTS.

vii

MAGELLAN;

OR, THE FIRST VOYAGE ROUND THE WORLD

CHAPTER I.

MAGELLAN GOES TO COURT.

NOT far from a quaint, picturesque old town in northern Portugal, called Villa Real, there lived, about the year 1500, a noble-man named Magellan. Although an "hidalgo," (nobleman) and descended from a proud and an-cient family, Magellan was not rich; but kept up such state and show as he could afford, in the home of his ancestors, which was a curious-look-ing edifice, with a tower, massive walls, and bat-tlements, and which became, in troublous times, a fortress, as well as a residence.

Here Magellan was wont to entertain the

neighboring hidalgos, to receive such distingished captains, nobles, or voyagers as wandered so far away from the capital, and to lord it over the peasants who tilled the fields and vineyards which stretched over the slopes of the not distant mountains, and along the fertile banks of the pretty stream that flowed between his estate and the town.

The pride of Magellan's heart was his son, Fernan; who, at the period that our story opens, was a vigorous young man of twenty. It was the custom of those days, as now, for the sons of European nobles to be brought up, not to any useful or hard-working occupation, but in ease and luxury; to be treated by their inferiors, even in earliest childhood, with ceremonious respect; and to devote themselves freely to vigorous sports, and such pleasures as their neighborhood or their opportunities afforded. There were but two callings which these young patricians usually thought worthy of their adoption. They were not too proud to become soldiers; and they were often glad to enter upon a political career, as courtiers or statesmen. At the time that Magellan lived, indeed, a third calling was espoused

by many young men of high birth; that of following the sea as voyagers and discoverers. But
this pursuit was nearly akin to that of a soldier.
The voyager commanded his ships upon the
ocean; but as soon as he had landed on a strange
shore, he buckled on his armor, donned his helmet, drew his sword, and led his men against the
inhabitants.

Although the elder Magellan was not rich,
young Fernan had been reared amid surround-
ings of comfort, petted and humored by his fond
father and equally doting mother, waited upon
obsequiously by the retainers of the house,
greeted with humble respect by the peasants
and village-folk wherever he made his appearance, and enjoying, to the full, the rough pleasures which the wild country round afforded.

The broad valley where he dwelt was almost
surrounded by lofty and savage mountains,
clothed with vast, luxuriant forests; while the
slopes that descended from it to the meadows
along the river bank, were covered by thickly
clustering vineyards, bearing the luscious purple
grapes from which the famous port wine is made.

Perhaps the chief pastime of Fernan's boyhood

and youth was the hunt. Among the mountains roamed the wild boar; the forests were, many of them, peopled with deer; while of smaller game there was an abundance; so that the sportsman need never despair of returning home with well-stocked game-bag, and often found his burden—a deer or a boar—too heavy to be carried without the aid of servants. It was Fernan's delight to follow his hounds, with a merry party of stalwart youths like himself, through the echoing mountain forests, and up the rugged banks of the sparkling river; to ride frantically in pursuit of the wild game, and come to close quarters with the fleet stags and tusk-gnashing boars; and to carry home in triumph the trophies of his day's sport.

Sometimes he encountered even more formidable foes than these; for the "Traz os Montes," near his home, were then infested by savage bands of brigands, who sought no richer prizes than the noble youths who ventured, in pursuit of game, too near their lairs. Fernan was as brave as a lion, and liked nothing better than a battle with the murderous robbers who now and then attacked him and his comrades. He had early learned the use of arms; and was a good swordsman, and a skilful shot. More than once he was brought in wounded from his struggles with the bandits; but he made light of his injuries, and had no sooner recovered than he plunged into the mountain wilds as fearlessly as before.

Not very many miles from the valley in which he dwelt, was Oporto, next to Lisbon the most important city in Portugal. It is from this city that "port" wine takes its name. Oporto is situated on the Atlantic, at the mouth of a wide river. It is a quaint old place, with narrow, zigzag streets, many ancient, lofty houses, adorned in the showy fashion of six or seven centuries ago, and possessing many noble churches and other public buildings. Its harbor is spacious, and to this day is picturesque with the ships of many nations.

In Fernan's time, Oporto was even a busier place than it now is. It was the resort of the nobility of all the country round, and its gaieties and dissipations were only less brilliant than those of Lisbon itself. The round of social pleasures was kept up there with much state and ceremony; while its trade, principally in wine, made the quays, and the region near them, very crowded and busy.

It was the custom of Fernan's father to spend, with his family, a portion of each year at Oporto; and there the young man had many a taste of the pleasures of city life. As he grew older, he became more and more fond of visiting the quays, and of taking sails in the harbor. He made the acquaintance of captains and sailors, and delighted to go on board the caravels and study their arrangements and rigging, and talk with the men about their adventures on the great deep. He would sit for hours in some dark cabin, and listen breathlessly to the tales of perilous voyages, of disastrous shipwrecks on strange coasts, and of desperate fights with savages. He heard with beating heart about the wonderful discoveries which were then being constantly made; about the exploits of Columbus, the heroic discovery of the way to India by his own countryman, Vasco da Gama, and the quick succeeding expeditions that now sailed between the old and the new world.

Of a bold, fearless, adventurous spirit, Fernan was soon seized with an intense passion for the sea. As he stood on the bustling quays of Oporto, and looked far out where rolled the mighty waves of the Atlantic, he wished that he, too, was a captain, and longed to try his fortune in strange lands. The pastimes of his country home now seemed to him dull and paltry; he said to himself that he was wasting his life, and that, instead of hunting boars and fighting brigands, he might be discovering new lands and winning renown like that of Columbus and da Gama. Even the exciting pleasures of the city—the bull-fights and masquerades, the tournaments and routs, began to pall upon him, and he pined to go out into the world, and see more of men and countries.

One day, when he had been thinking more seriously than usual about his present life, and yearning to change it for a more stirring one, he sought his father in the hall of the house, where the bluff old noble sat, warming his heels before a blazing log-fire.

As he approached, Magellan observed that the young man's brows were knit, and that his face wore a serious and thoughtful expression.

"What troubles you, Fernan?" asked the

hidalgo. "For some time you have seemed distraught, as if something had happened to perplex you. Sit here by me, son, and open your heart to me."

Fernan did as he was bidden, and after a moment, said: "It is true, my father, that I am not content. I no longer enjoy those pastimes and pleasures that were once my delight. I thirst for adventure, for a stirring life by land and sea. You see, sir, I am now a man, I would go forth into the world, and try my fortune."

"And that shall you, if you please!" said the old man. "To be sure, Traz os Montes is but a dull place for one so brave and ambitious as you; and even Oporto is but a narrow field for your aspirations. You shall go to court, my lad, and seek the favor of our good King Manuel. It will be ill luck if he does not speedily find some exploit for you; I warrant me, a stalwart youth like you will find merit in his royal eyes."

Fernan sprang joyfully to his feet, and seized and kissed his father's hand. "You fill me with happiness, my father!" he exclaimed. "Nothing do I desire so much as to go to Lisbon, and see the splendors of the court, and take service with the king! Think you, sir, that he will receive me in his household? And may it be, that I shall be sent ere long, on some glorious expedition of conquest and discovery? I long to ride the stormy billows, to match my prowess with savage hosts, to win a name and power! When may I go—shall it be soon, my lord?"

"In what haste are you, Fernan, to leave home and kindred!" replied the old man, sorrowfully. "But you have an impetuous soul, and mayhap nothing will content you but to go forth into the world. King Manuel knows me, and knows that he hath no more sturdy or loyal subject. I doubt not, he will receive you on my petition. Go, then; prepare with such haste as you please; and depart for Lisbon as soon as you are ready."

It was with light, brisk step that Fernan, after thanking his father with trembling voice for his goodness, left the hall, and repaired to his own room, in an upper story of the house. A glow of high spirits already suffused his face, but just now so long-drawn with discontent; and as he paced up and down the floor, with a multitude of feverishly happy thoughts rushing through his brain, his eyes kindled, and his fists clenched in his excitement. Now and then he broke out into some warlike ballad, or some sailor's song, that he had heard in the barracks, or on the caravels at Oporto; and then, becoming calmer, he would look around the room, to see what he could carry with him to the royal court.

There were many preparations to make before he could set out for Lisbon. In order to appear properly at court, a young nobleman must have several suits of rich attire. He must have tunics and trousers of velvet and silk, trimmed with gold and silver lace; he must have slashed caps, with high-nodding plumes; he must have a full suit of glistening armor, helmet, cuirass, buckler, and all; he must have an ample supply of silk stockings, of velvet shoes and slippers, and long top-boots; he must wear a sword, with chased and jewelled hilt and scabbard; he must be supplied with arquebuses and daggers and belts; and, not least, he must be provided with at least one high-mettled, thorough-bred steed, on which to prance and gallop at the state shows and processions. In providing himself with these things, Fernan now busied himself absorbingly during his waking hours. Tailors stitched away unceasingly on his fine new clothes; the hidalgo sent to a distance, and purchased a noble, milk-white horse, for there were none in his stables fit for so momentous a use; and ere many weeks Fernan found himself splendidly equipped for his journey to Lisbon.

One bright morning, there was a lively bustle in the courtyard of his father's mansion at Villa Real. The hidalgo himself, richly dressed, and surrounded by his wife, sons and daughters, stood on the broad steps that led from the door to the paved court, while the servants were gathered in groups below. Presently Fernan's white horse, with gay trappings, was brought out; and then Fernan himself appeared, very fine, in a bran-new suit, with plumed cap, and a sword hanging at his side. With him were to go attendants, who soon cantered in the courtyard on their steeds.

The moment of parting came; and Fernan advancing to his parents, knelt to receive their blessing, and was fondly folded in their arms. He embraced in turn his brothers and sisters, waved an adieu to the retainers of the household who gathered to see him off; and, springing lightly upon his horse's back, rode forth, followed by his attendants, on his way to Lisbon.

It took several days to traverse the highways that led from Villa Real to the capital of the kingdom. Fernan's journey was, however, through a smiling and fruitful country, where the vineyards grew luxuriantly, and were just now laden with luscious ripe grapes of many colors. At night, he put up at a wayside inn, where he occupied the best room the house afforded, and regaled himself right merrily on the ragouts and omelets which were served up to him smoking hot, with his wine and biscuits. Everywhere he was received with the honor due to his rank and his destined position at court; nor did any accident befall him until, on an Autumn afternoon, his eyes were gladdened by the sight of Lisbon in the distance.

On reaching the capital, and after taking quarters at a hotel which stood not far from the royal palace, Fernan lost no time in seeking an audience of King Manuel. This was easy enough to obtain. Among the young courtiers, Fernan found several old friends from his own part of the country; and they found no difficulty in introducing him to the royal presence.

King Manuel was still youthful, and carried himself with truly royal grace and dignity. His face
was rather a stern one, but bore upon it the impress of a grave and thoughtful, rather than an
ill-natured character. Ambitious, and eager to
advance the glory and power of his realm, and to
outvie its rival, Spain, in the conquest and dominion of distant lands, he was an ardent stu-
dent, and employed his time rather in serious
affairs of state than in the frivolous gaieties of
court life.

The monarch was seated in the great hall of
his palace, surrounded by his courtiers and officers, when Fernan, arrayed in his most brilliant
suit, was ushered into his presence.

"The son of the hidalgo Magellan is right welcome," said King Manuel, as Fernan bowed low
before him; "and it will please me to give him
a place in my household." With that, the king
went on to inform Fernan that his duty would
be to attend the royal person, that he should
have a certain stipend every month with which
to maintain himself, and that he should be provided with an apartment in the palace.

In no long time, Fernan had become com-

pletely accustomed to court life. The fine
dresses, the brilliant displays, the balls and par
ties, the great dinners and imposing ceremonies,
for awhile amused and distracted him. He enjoyed the city, with its busy streets, its crowded
roadstead, its fine buildings, its gay life; and not
less, the companionship of many young men of
his own rank and age, with whom he passed many
a jolly and boisterous hour.

But his ambition was by no means satisfied
by these pastimes and pleasures. The court to
him was only the high road to a more stirring
and manly career. As he saw the fleets of caravels sail out of the harbor, on their way to newly
found lands in Africa, Asia, and America, he
longed, too, to traverse the seas, and seek the
glories of combat, and the still nobler glories of
discovery. Impatiently he watched the preparations of his more lucky companions, who were
chosen to take part in these expeditions; he
chafed under the necessity by which, while they
went forth in search of adventures, he was still
bound by his service to the king.

Meanwhile, he grew in the royal favor. King
Manuel, perceiving him to be more aspiring and

more serious than many of his fellow-courtiers,
kept him about his own person, and often engaged
in conversation with him.   Fernan attracted the
king's good will by the enthusiasm with which
he talked of the discoveries which had been made
by the Portuguese voyagers; and in his own
mind, the king soon marked him out as one
likely in the not distant future, to be of important service to the state.   Had Don Manuel continued to esteem Fernan so highly, he would
have added one more bright jewel to his crown,
in the possession of the famous straits, the discovery of which is to be described in the following pages; but, unfortunately for Portugal, in the
course of time he took a dislike to the ambitious
young man, and Spain, instead of Portugal, reaped
the benefit of his rare genius.

CHAPTER II.

MAGELLAN AT THE WARS.

FERNAN had not been long at court, when an event occurred which threw Lisbon into excitement, and which was destined to turn the current of Fernan's future life. This was the return of the famous discoverer, Vasco da Gama, from his second voyage to India.

The victories which da Gama had gained, his successful voyages to and from India, the splendid reception with which he was welcomed home, the honors of nobility and fortune that were showered upon him, the praises of him that rang through Portugal, all excited Fernan's ambition, and stimulated anew his longing to enter upon a career of adventure. In no long time he made Vasco da Gama's acquaintance, and was soon admitted to his intimacy; and many an hour did the young man spend at da Gama's house, listening

to the soul-stirring tales of his exploits by sea
and land. Da Gama told him of the marvellous
riches of India; of the customs of the people,
and the struggles in which they had engaged
with the Portuguese; and in such glowing colors
described the romance of that distant land, the
perils which there awaited the Portuguese warriors,
and the glories which they might achieve, that
Fernan burned to take part in its further conquest.

There was then at the Portuguese court, a
brave and enterprising captain, named Francisco
D'Almeyda. He had won renown at the famous
seige of Granada, and in fighting the Moors in
Africa; and he was descended from one of the
noblest families of Portugal. King Manuel had
no more courageous or courtly subject.

Some time after Vasco da Gama's return,
D'Almeyda was chosen as the first viceroy, or
governor of India. So much loved and trusted
was he, that no sooner was his approaching departure for the East announced, than a crowd
of seekers after adventure, of all ranks and con-
ditions, flocked to him and begged to be allowed
to go with him.

D'Almeyda knew Fernan Magellan, whom he had long been in the habit of meeting about the court. He had seen more than one instance of his bravery, and was deeply impressed with the restless ardor of his ambition. No sooner did Fernan, therefore, appear before him, and eagerly ask for a place under his command, than the viceroy freely promised him what he desired.

Fernan now set eagerly about his preparations for departure. He besought and easily obtained the consent of King Manuel; and finding that he had plenty of spare time before D'Almeyda sailed, he employed it in revisiting his home in Traz os Montes, to bid adieu to his parents, brothers and sisters, and take a last look at the familiar scenes of his childhood. He was going a long way off, into the midst of many dangers, and might never behold those beloved haunts again.

He was in the flower of young manhood, being about twenty-five years of age, when, from the deck of the flag-ship of D'Almeyda's fleet, he saw, with contending emotions, the shores of Portugal growing dim and fading away in the distance. He found himself at last a soldier, in a large and well-appointed force; and he was impatient that

the voyage should be rapidly pursued, and that
they should quickly reach the scene of their
future exploits.

No untoward mishap marked the progress of
the fleet. Gentle winds wafted it on its course;
scarcely a gale assailed it as it sped on, touching
now at the Cape Verde Islands, now at the pretty
harbor at St. Helena, and at last near the Cape
of Good Hope.

D'Almeyda's first task was to secure Portuguese garrisons at certain points on the East
African coast, where, according to the reports that
had reached King Manuel, there was an abundance of gold and other riches. Entering the
harbor of Quiloa, a town on the coast ruled over
by a barbarian king who was hostile to the Portuguese, he assailed, captured, and plundered it.
Fernan here had his first taste of the excitements
and dangers of battle, and side-by-side with his
noble commander, he fought with a headlong
and lion-like courage which at once marked him
out as a hero among his comrades.

From Quiloa, where he built a fort, D'Almeyda
went to Mombaza, further up the coast; and
here, too, the Portuguese met with a stout re-

sistance from the natives. These natives had already had a taste of European warfare; for some years before Vasco da Gama had attacked them. He had, it seems, lost some of his cannon overboard. These the natives had managed to haul up from the bottom of the sea; and, somehow, they had learned how to use them; so that, when D'Almeyda assailed them, he was amazed to be welcomed with the roar of artillery. He succeeded, however, after a desperate fight, in capturing Mombaza, where he found an abundance of spoil; and he remained in this place some days.

One morning, as Fernan was looking about him in this strange African town, he was surprised to see, propped up near the gate of the palace, a large iron anchor. On examining it further, he found that it had, without doubt, come from Portugal. He hastened to report the discovery to D'Almeyda; who, on questioning some of the natives, learned that it was an anchor which Vasco da Gama had lost in the harbor, and which had been hauled up, and by order of the king, placed at his palace gate as a curiosity.

The next place at which the fleet stopped was

the friendly town of Melinda, where Vasco da
Gama had been welcomed and treated with lavish
hospitality. The old king, who had shown him
so much attention, was dead; but in his stead
ruled his son, who proved equally well-disposed
towards the Portuguese. D'Almeyda was received
with cordial greeting, visited the king in his flourishing city, and was allowed to build a fort on the
heights that rose above it.

All this time, the fleet had been gradually
drawing nearer to India, its final destination; and
on leaving Melinda, it struck directly across the
ocean, favored by the trade winds, and after a
rapid voyage, reached Malabar.

Fernan, who had shown conspicuous bravery in
all the battles in which the Portuguese had been
engaged with the Africans, and had become
a great favorite, both with D'Almeyda and with
his fellow-soldiers, was delighted to see at last
the land of which he had heard so much, and
where he hoped to fight his way up to fame
and fortune. He gazed in wonder at the singular
costumes of the natives, the gorgeous turbans
and tunics that adorned the persons of the princes
and great men, the bazaars, full of rich cloths,

fine carvings, and luscious fruits; and marvelled at the luxurious vegetation that crowned the hills and clustered in the valleys.

But he was soon called away from all this sight-seeing, by his duties as a soldier. He had not come merely to visit a strange land, and idly observe its curiosities and customs. There was stern work before him; and he cheerily obeyed the summons that called upon him to follow his commander.

He served gallantly with D'Almeyda in his many attacks upon the Indian chiefs and towns that still resisted the Portuguese sway; went with him to Cochin and Cananore, took part in the desperate seige of Coulam, and that of Onor, and engaged in many a fight with the Moors, who, jealous of the Portuguese, exerted their utmost energies to drive them from India.

It happened that, after Fernan had been in India some time, a famous Portuguese general, Alfonso de Albuquerque, arrived with a large force, with the purpose of carrying the conquests of Portugal still further east. Albuquerque was one of the greatest soldiers of his time. He had a noble nature, was refined, generous, energetic, and as brave a man as there was in the world. His soldiers idolized him, because, though very stern when offended, he cheerfully shared their hardships, and always led them in person. He had a pleasant, genial face, which was rendered yet more benign by the long, snow-white beard that fell over his breast, almost to his waist; his eye was bright and kindly, but in battle was lit up with the fierce fire of his valor and enthusiasm; his bearing was at once dignified and gracious.

To Albuquerque, Fernan was at once attracted, and, as D'Almeyda was now busy with the civil affairs of his viceroyalty, and matters were, for the time, quiet in India, he hastened to enlist under Albuquerque's standard.

Near the straits between the Indian Ocean and the Persian gulf lies an island, on which stood, and still stands, the city of Ormuz. It is an old saying in the East, that "the world is a ring, and Ormuz is the gem set in it." At the time of which we speak, Ormuz was, in consequence of its position as commanding the straits between the two oceans, one of the most important places in all Asia. Its harbor was always full of the quaint craft of the Eastern waters; Arabian, Moorish, Persian, Indian, Malay, Tartar, and Armenian boats might have been seen crowded together in its roadstead; while its markets teemed with the various wares produced in the countries to which they belonged. The city itself was alive with trade; its streets and squares were spread over a wide area; and it possessed many stately buildings.

The Portuguese had long looked with covetous eyes upon so fine a military position, and so rich an emporium; and Albuquerque was resolved to add this " gem of the world" to the crown of his royal master.

It was in September, 1507, that he set sail, with a fleet of seven ships and a force of less than five hundred men, to attack a city which, he knew well, was defended by a large garrison of Indians and Persians. With Albuquerque went, his heart aglow with excitement and hope, Fernan Magellan. There was not a soldier in the little army that looked forward more cheerily than he to what was nothing less than a recklessly audacious en-terprise. His experience in war made him con-fident of his prowess; and he longed to meet foemen, like the Persians and Arabs, more worthy of the steel of Portuguese cavaliers than the African barbarians and the half-civilized Hindoos.

In due time the fleet arrived off the busy harbor of Ormuz; and Albuquerque hastened to attack the ships which defended it. One by one the native ships, riddled by Albuquerque's cannon, sank beneath the waves; the town itself was set on fire; and soon a message came from the grand vizier, that he would yield to the Portuguese, acknowledge King Manuel as the lord of Ormuz, allow a fort to be built, and pay a large tribute. Content with this submission, Albuquerque sailed back to India again.

But when he had gone, the vizier, (who was reigning as regent in Ormuz, during the infancy of its prince), refused to fulfill his pledges; and the next year, Albuquerque again attacked the city. This time he was badly repulsed; and was at last forced to give up the purpose of capturing it.

In these conflicts young Fernan took an eager and gallant part. More than once he fell seriously wounded, but as soon as his wounds were dressed, he was up again, fighting with all his might; and soon was known throughout India as one of the bravest captains in the Portuguese camp.

He went on many of the expeditions that were undertaken by Albuquerque and other generals, everywhere displaying conspicuous valor and military skill; and he at the same time made himself beloved by his fellow-soldiers, by sharing their dangers and hardships, and devoting himself heart and soul to their welfare.

On one occasion, a small fleet was sent by Albuquerque from Cochin back to Portugal, and two ships, one of them commanded by Magellan, were dispatched to convey this fleet into the open sea. These two ships set out towards night; but had not proceeded far, when, in the darkness, they both struck on the shoals of Padua, remaining aground, and upright on their keels. It was a situation of great peril, for the ships were likely to break up and founder at any moment. In all haste the boats were got out, and a great clamor now arose among the men as to who should return in them to the main land.

At this critical juncture, Magellan displayed the true nobility of his nature. Although, as an officer, he was entitled to return in the boats, he resolutely refused to do so. He declared that he would remain with the men, while the rest of the officers went back; and he went around among the sailors, exhorting them to stand by the ships as long as they remained above water.

His example put to shame those who had been clamoring to return to the main land, and his cheery words turned their terror into confidence.

He happened, just as one of the boats, full of its human freight, was about to pull away to the shore, to step into it for a moment, to speak to its captain. One of the sailors, alarmed at this, cried out to him:

"Sir, did you not promise to stay with us?"

"Yes," shouted back Magellan; "and see, I am coming;" with which he climbed back upon the stranded ship again, and took his place among those who were to stay by the ships.

The boats having departed, Magellan set vigorously to work to save the ships and their cargoes. He ordered shores to be set with the yards on each side of the vessels, their sides to be raised as well as possible, and biscuits and water to be put within. These tasks done, Magellan saw to it that the men committed no rob-

beries, and completely won their confidence by
the promptness and vigor of his measures.

In this dangerous situation the crew remained
for a week; when some caravels, sent out to suc-
cor them, arrived, took them on board, and
transferred so much of the cargoes as remained
uninjured by the salt water. The stranded ships
were then burned, and Magellan and his companions returned safely to Cochin.

Soon after this, Magellan committed an act
which not only deprived him of the affection of
Albuquerque, but had a very important influence
on his future career. He was now one of the
most distinguished of the Portuguese captains in
Portugal, and was called into the councils of the
viceroy and the generals, to take part in the
decisions which those councils made.

Albuquerque was anxious to make an attack
on a town called Goa, which was situated on an
island, just off the coast of India. It had a good
harbor, and was one of the chief trading-places
on the coast. He therefore called a council of
war, and proposed his project to the assembled
chiefs. Among these was Magellan. On hearing the general's plan, he was bold enough to

oppose it. He reminded Albuquerque that the winds were now contrary, and that if the ships were taken to Goa, they could not return that year to Portugal; and did his utmost to dissuade the general from the expedition.

Magellan's opposition did not please Albuquerque, who, though not an unamiable man, was impatient of contradiction. He declared that in spite of what Magellan said, he should go to Goa, with such ships as he had, and such men as chose to go with him; and he accordingly sailed out of Cochin with twenty-one vessels, and sixteen hundred soldiers, to execute his purpose.

Having thus displeased the old warrior, under whose lead he had fought so long and well, Magellan found himself out of service in India. But he could not rest idle. His ambition still stirred him to attempt deeds of daring, to share the the thrilling perils of the camp and field.

Besides alienating the good will of Albuquerque, he had lost nearly all the property he had acquired during his residence in India; and to continue his military life was not only a satisfaction but a necessity.

He accordingly turned his eyes to another part

of the world, where the Portuguese were contend
ing for dominion, just as they were in India.
They had long engaged in fierce wars with the
Moors; and had managed to secure some foot.
hold in Morocco. Thither Magellan, pining for
active service, wended his way; and soon found
himself in command of some Portuguese troops
at a settlement called Azamor. Here he engaged
in almost continual conflicts with the Moors and
Arabs, who struggled fiercely against the European intruders upon African soil.

Magellan would sally out from the town, at
the head of a body of his brave troopers, and recklessly assail the Arab camps that threatened to
attack it. He rode or marched at the head of his
soldiers, and was the first to fire at or cut down
with sword the swarthy foes who rushed out to
meet him.

On one of these rash sallies, Magellan fell
hotly upon an Arab camp, and was dealing Herculean blows, right and left, when a poisoned javelin,
hurled from the midst of the enemy, entered his
leg. He had so often been wounded before, that
he made light of the circumstance; but on being
carried back to Azamor, it was found that the

Magellan wounded.   Page 30.

wound was a serious one. The skill of the sur-
geons soon restored him to health; but from that
day till his death, Magellan was lame.

Magellan, through all the exciting events in
which he had taken part since leaving the royal
court at Lisbon, had never lost sight of the chief
ambition and desire of his youth. This was, to
win the laurels of a great discoverer, and to
leave his name renowned in history, as were
those of Columbus and Vasco da Gama. He had
now seen much service, and felt that there was
little glory to be gained in the petty wars with
the Moors; and he became impatient to enter
upon some long and hazardous voyage, and
search the strange and obscure regions of the
world.

He therefore repaired to Lisbon, to entreat
King Manuel to fit up and give him the command
of an expedition of discovery.

CHAPTER III.

MAGELLAN IN SPAIN.

MAGELLAN approached the capital of his native land with much misgiving. He knew but too well that King Manuel no longer looked upon him with the favor he once had done, in spite of his heroic service in India and Africa. His resistance to Albuquerque's plans had been reported to the court, and had deeply offended the king. Moreover, when Magellan, finding his stipend too little to support him, had petitioned the king to increase it, the request had been curtly refused.

Yet he was resolved not to waste his years in fighting against the Moors. He had heard, from one of his most intimate friends, an energetic voyager named Francisco Serrano, of the delights and riches of the famous Molucca Islands, in the Eastern seas ; and, after deep study of the rude

maps which then existed, Magellan came to the
conclusion that those islands might be reached
by sailing, not southward and eastward, by the
Cape of Good Hope and around India, but westward, across the Atlantic.

If this were only possible to be done, he who
should succeed in doing it would win renown
rivalling that of Vasco da Gama himself; and
Magellan made up his mind that, at all hazards,
he would attempt it.

On reaching Lisbon, he lost no time in seeking
an audience of King Manuel. But the king,
having now imbibed a violent prejudice against his
brave officer, at first refused to see him at all;
and Magellan's heart sank within him.

One day, however, he received a summons to
appear in the royal presence. Determined to
make the best of circumstances, Magellan donned
a rich suit of velvet, put on a handsome cap
adorned with plumes, and taking his handsomest
sword from the wall, buckled it about his waist.
Then, with haughty carriage, for even before
majesty itself he would bear himself proudly, he
entered the audience chamber, and advanced
with a slight limp in his gait, to where the king

sat upon his throne, surrounded by his courtiers.

King Manuel glanced at him coldly, and a frown gathered on his face.

"Well, sir," said he, sternly, "why have you left your post in Africa, to come hither? What petition do you desire to make?"

"I have come, your Majesty," replied Magellan, bowing, "to ask for an employment higher and more perilous, and of greater benefit to your throne, than that in which I have been engaged. I pray you to reflect, sir, that I have been of some service to the state. My wounds, that I bear on every part of my body, attest it. I seek a wider field of service to your Majesty."

"Magellan," was the royal retort, "you caused sore trouble in India, when you obstinately opposed the projects of my good general, Albuquerque, and incited the captains to refuse to go with him; you have demanded of me a larger stipend than you deserve; and you have left your post to come hither on some fool's errand. What do you wish?"

"The king is not just to me!" boldly declared the cavalier. "But I will not dare reproach him. Sire, my wish is to command an expedition of discovery. I would seek a new and shorter way, by sailing westward, to the islands of the eastern seas."

"It is folly!" said the king, "I will not permit you to attempt it. Retire, Magellan. You have provoked my displeasure by leaving your post. Return to it, sir, and be thankful that you are not punished for your conduct."

With bowed head, and countenance deadly pale with indignation and disappointment, Magellan slowly passed out of the hall into the corridor of the palace. Overcome with sad emotion, he leaned against one of the pillars, and almost sobbed in his intense grief. Thus were all his bright hopes dashed ; thus all his bright dreams of adventures and fame rudely dispelled.

As he lingered in the corridor, a tall, stalwart man, with black beard that swept down to his girdle, his body enveloped in a long black gown, and his head covered with a black velvet skullcap, approached, and gently laid his hand upon the cavalier's shoulder.

"Be of good cheer, Magellan!" said he, in a low, sympathetic voice. "There are other kings in Christendom besides King Manuel, and other

stout and goodly caravels than those of Portugal.
All is not lost because your petition is rejected.
You have been severely treated; but if King
Manuel blindly refuses to perceive your genius,
there are those who will!"

"What mean you, my friend?" asked Magellan, looking up with a bright glance in his eyes,
for the other's words gave him a world of encour-
agement, and comfort; " what career is open to
me, besides that which King Manuel refuses?"

"Why, that which his rival, King Charles, will
open to you! Know you not that the Spanish
king is ambitious, and is jealous of the triumphs
of Portugal on the sea, and her conquests in distant lands?"

"What, Faleiro," exclaimed Magellan, "would
you have me desert my native land, and my sovereign, to seek a foreign service?"

"Nothing is more common," replied the other.
" Here, your service is disdainfully rejected. To
stay, is to spend your life in stupid skirmishes
with Moors and Arabs, to live on a miserable
pittance. If King Manuel will have none of you,
in what are you bound to him?"

Faleiro's words sank deep into Magellan's heart.

They revived his faltering hopes, and opened before him a new prospect, just as that which had so much allured him seemed closed forever. His soul smarted under the sharp reproofs and abrupt refusal of King Manuel; his pride was wounded to the quick; his nature revolted from humble submission to the disgrace of being thus publicly and scornfully repelled.

Taking Faleiro's arm, he walked with him slowly out of the palace, towards his friend's lodgings.

This Faleiro was an astrologer, and professed to read the future in the stars and signs of the heavens. Astrologers in those days were held in great honor and reverence in Spain and Portugal; and even the wisest men lent an eager ear to their prophecies. So it was that Faleiro was highly esteemed at King Manuel's court. It was there that he had learned to love the impetuous and warm-hearted Magellan; and as he himself had a taste for travel and adventures, they soon became very intimate.

The astrologer had heard with both sorrow and anger the king's harsh words to Magellan; and he now devoted himself to reviving the downcast spirits of his friend.

They soon reached Faleiro's abode. It was a plain, somewhat gloomy building; and this impression was increased when one entered the dark apartment where the astrologer pursued his mysterious studies.

The unpainted walls were hung with astronomical charts, and strange pictures representing various aspects of the firmament; while on the long tables that lined the room were globes, telescopes, and other instruments used by Faleiro in his nightly tasks. A plain table occupied the centre, and to this two high-backed chairs were drawn.

It being now dusk, Faleiro lighted a taper, which spread a dim light through the apartment: and motioning to Magellan to sit in one chair, himself took possession of the other.

"The present is dark to you, dear Fernan," he said; "it seems to you, does it not, as if no bright future were in store for you?"

"Do you bid me hope," was Magellan's reply, "for better fortune?"

"I do. You know that I have cast your horoscope, and have predicted for you a great and glorious career. In your own land you have nothing to hope for. Go, therefore, to Spain; the king will recognize your merits, and, no doubt, will give you a fleet. If you will go, Fernan, I will go with you. I, too, long to brave the ocean's perils, to search out new countries. We will seek our fortune on the deep together."

His friend's declaration that he would go with him decided Magellan. He no longer hesitated, but said that he would lose no time in preparing to change his allegiance from Don Manuel to King Charles. It was late at night when the friends parted with warm embraces. Magellan hastened to his lodgings, and tossed all night on his bed, agitated by the new project that filled his mind. The more he thought of it, the more firmly fixed became his resolve to leave the service of his ungrateful sovereign, and to become a subject of the king of Spain. As Faleiro had said, it was no uncommon thing then (nor is it now) for a man to thus transfer his citizenship and adopt another country than that in which he had been born; and Magellan certainly had the strongest reason to abandon his allegiance to King Manuel.

There was another reason, of which he had

said nothing to Faleiro, why the project of going
to Spain pleased him.

At Seville lived a cousin of his, named Don
Diego Barbosa. This Barbosa was a man of
much wealth and importance, and although a
Portuguese, had risen to be mayor of the ancient
Spanish city. He lived in a grand house there,
and gave splendid entertainments, and lived in
sumptuous luxury.

Before Barbosa had moved from Lisbon to
Seville, young Magellan had been in the habit of
visiting familiarly at his house. He had been
received, being a relation, as one of the family ;
and many of the pleasantest hours of his early
sojourn at court, were spent at his cousin
Barbosa's.

Of one member of the family, Magellan became especially fond. This was Barbosa's lovely
young daughter, Beatrix. She was tall and slight,
with long, rich, raven ringlets, melting brown eyes,
and gentle and graceful bearing. No wonder that
the young courtier was dazzled by her beauty, or
that she, in return, was pleased with the fine
cavalier who cast upon her so many soft, appeal-
ing glances.

When Barbosa, carrying away the fair Beatrix, repaired to Seville to live, Magellan was very much cast down. But soon after, he had sailed for India, and his grief at losing sight of his lovely cousin, was softened amid the stirring scenes which absorbed his mind in the East.

Now, he was himself going to Spain, and would not fail to visit Seville. Then, if Beatrix were still free, he would revive his courtship, and win her if he could.

In no long time, the two friends had made their preparations for departure. Magellan resigned his commission as an officer in King Manuel's army; and without taking the trouble to make his appearance again at a court where he had been so rudely and publicly disgraced, set out on horseback, with Faleiro, for Seville.

The journey was a long one, but the travellers were not pressed for time, and made merry on their bright prospects, as they went. Fortunately, they had a good supply of money, and were attended by two faithful servants, who went fully armed, lest the party should be attacked by the brigands.

It was mid-Autumn, and nature was brilliant

with the fast-changing foliage of the dense forests
of Southern Portugal and Spain. Everywhere,
in the vineyards, the grape-pickers, of all ages and
both sexes, were busily at work, gathering the
full-ripe harvest ; while ever and anon the travellers came upon the yards where, in rude stone
troughs, the peasants were busy treading and
pressing the grapes, the juice of which ran out,
in gushing streams, into the big tubs set below.
Magellan and Faleiro often stopped to pass a
merry word with the toilers, and to drink the
new-made wine, as they sat at the tables in front
of the cozy wayside inns.

They reached Seville without mishap, and repaired at once to a large hostelry, which stood on
one of the public squares. Magellan's heart beat
high as he thought that, not far off, lived
Beatrix, all unconscious that he was so near. A
hundred doubts and misgivings passed through
his excited mind. Perhaps she was already
married ; perhaps she had entirely forgotten him ;
perhaps, true to her love, but despairing of his,
she had retired to a convent, and become a nun.
Many years had passed since he had seen her ;
and, instead of the slim, shy girl of fourteen that

he so tenderly remembered, she must now be a stately and mature woman of twenty-five.

Eager as he was, however, to see her and learn his fate, his thoughts were not entirely absorbed by the gentle Beatrix. He reflected with a thrill that he was now in the territory of the war-like and ambitious king of Spain ; that he was within a step of those famous quays of Seville, whence so many gallant expeditions had sailed in search of discovery, and where, even now, fleets of caravels lay at anchor, ready to make their ventures upon the ocean. Magellan longed to stroll along the quays, and to talk with the rough captains about their expected voyages.

Arrayed in his gayest attire, Magellan set out the next day to make known his presence in Seville, to his cousin, Diego Barbosa. He approached the spacious mansion with fluttering heart, and his hand trembled as he knocked upon its lofty portal.

Don Diego received him with the warmest welcome. He had heard, with pride, of Magellan's exploits in India and Africa, and was delighted to learn that he now proposed to enter King Charles's service. He bade Magellan make his house his home, and ordered the best that his well-stocked larder afforded to be set before the new-comer.

To Magellan's anxious inquiries for Beatrix, Don Diego replied that she was at home, and well, and that he should presently judge how she was, for himself.

He had, indeed, scarcely finished the bounteous meal which his cousin had caused to be set before him, when Beatrix entered. She had grown, as he supposed, to be a charming and graceful woman; and to his joy, he perceived that she welcomed him with the same blushing warmth that she used to do. It was a moment of rare delight to the lovers when they found that, after so long a separation, each retained the old affection for the other.

Magellan at once took up his quarters at Don Diego's; and made up for the lost time in his eager courtship of Beatrix. Her father, far from being averse to this state of things, encouraged it; and ere long Magellan had pleaded for and won the hand of his fair cousin, with the Don's full consent and blessing.

While his friend was thus revelling in the delights of happy love, Faleiro busied himself with the errand on which he had come to Spain. He made the acquaintance of many captains, and sought for some time in vain, for an opportunity to lay their projects before the king. Meanwhile, he petitioned to the Council of India, a body of grandees who had charge of the Spanish possessions and discoveries in the East, to accept their services, and send them on an expedition to find the way, by a westward route, to the Molucca Islands.

Four months after their arrival at Seville, Magellan and Faleiro set out for Valladolid, where the royal court was sojourning. They were attended by a large retinue of servants, provided for them by the good Don Diego; and as they passed along the highway between Seville and Valladolid, they met many cavalcades passing to and from the court. The Spanish knights who met Magellan greeted him with respect and honor, for his fame had reached King Charles's dominions, and it had gradually been whispered abroad that he was about to enter the Spanish service.

On reaching Valladolid, they found, to their disappointment, that the king was away in the north, on a hunting expedition; but they were reassured by the favorable reception with which Fonseca, the president of the Council of India, welcomed them at court.

They lost no time in laying their plans before this great man. He listened incredulously, and when Magellan, with earnest voice and excited gestures, tried to show him, by a chart, how it was as possible to pass around the South American Continent, as it had been for Vasco da Gama to double the Cape of Good Hope, he smilingly shook his head. Fonseca, however, promised that as soon as the king returned, he would secure an audience for the two Portuguese; and they waited impatiently until Charles should be surfeited with his hunting, and should reappear in the midst of his court.

CHAPTER IV.

PREPARATIONS FOR THE VOYAGE.

KING CHARLES of Spain, at the time that Magellan sought him at Valladolid, was scarcely more than a boy in years; but already he betrayed the bold and ambitious traits which were to make him famous, when after-wards, as the Emperor Charles V. of Germany, he engaged in the great wars with France.

At the age of eighteen, though beardless, slight, and short in form, with a head of thick, stubby, yellow hair, and the large jaw of the royal house of Castile, there was something in his presence and bearing that was not only kingly, but that inspired all who approached him with a respect which was as much a tribute to his character as to his rank.

Charles was especially earnest in his desire to

maintain and increase the renown of Spain as the discoverer and conquerer of distant lands. He was proud of the noble traditions of Ferdinand and Isabella, his grandfather and grandmother; rejoiced to remember that it was by their help that Columbus was enabled to find a new continent beyond the Atlantic; and was deeply jealous of the triumphs of his neighbors, the Portuguese, in their conquests in India, and on the African coast.

When Magellan and Faleiro, therefore, were ushered into his presence, the king was prepared to give them a hearty welcome, and to listen with attentive ear to what they said.

In presence of the Spanish court, Magellan unfolded his project in an earnest and eloquent speech. He described to the king the discoveries already made in America, and declared that, if he were only permitted to make the attempt, he had no doubt of being able to find a passage around the newly-discovered continent. His enthusiasm at once inspired King Charles with confidence in him; and his words, describing in glowing terms the increased wealth and power which would come to the Spanish crown, if his proposed voyage were successful, aroused all Charles's eager ambition.

On being dismissed from the royal presence, Magellan and Faleiro returned to their lodgings, to await, in anxious suspense, the king's decision. His gracious bearing towards them led them to hope that he would grant their wishes; nor was this hope disappointed.

A few days after, they received a summons to appear before Fonseca, the president of the Council of India; and when they entered his apartment, he welcomed them with a cordiality which augured well for their project. His words soon relieved them of all doubt.

"The king," he said, "has well considered what you said to him; and has consulted his grandees and counsellors upon the matter. He decides to consent to your desires; to furnish you with a fleet, of which you, Magellan, are to have the command; and trusting in your loyalty, he will provide you with the men and materials necessary for your expedition."

The friends embraced each other in their joy, and warmly expressed their gratitude to Fonseca. Once more Magellan's heart beat with proud and ambitious anticipation. The chief longing of his life was about to be gratified. He would at last traverse the ocean, and search for the passage, the existence which had been a deeply-seated belief in his soul.

Full of exultation, he dispatched a messenger with a letter for his beloved Beatrix at Seville, which apprized her of his glorious success at court; and then, with Faleiro, cheerily set to work preparing for the expedition that had so long filled his thoughts.

King Charles was as good as his word. He agreed to fit out five sound and sturdy ships, and to man them with two hundred and fifty able seamen, who should be paid, for a period of two years, out of the royal treasury of Spain. He promised Magellan that, if he succeeded in discovering the desired passage, no other Spanish seaman should go through it for ten years; that he should have command of the fleet as its admiral, and be the governor of all the lands that he might discover.

The king further agreed that Magellan should have a twentieth part of all the revenues from these lands, which the Spanish treasury received;

that he should be allowed to send cargoes of spices to Spain every year, to the value of one thousand ducats, a fifth of which he should have for himself; and that, of the islands he should discover, after the king had chosen six, he should have, as his own, the seventh and eighth.

Thus, if the voyage were only successful, Magellan would not only win great fame, but become speedily a rich man; for the islands in the seas to which he hoped to penetrate were well known to be teeming with precious spices and other valuable productions.

But Magellan's path was not yet an altogether smooth one. Many Spanish courtiers and captains became jealous of the foreigner's success with the king, and whispered suspicions into the royal ear. It was an outrage, they said, for a Portuguese to be put in command of a Spanish fleet, and to reap the honors due to the faithful subjects of the crown. There were many Spaniards, they declared, who were as able and as eager as Magellan to undertake the voyage; and this task should have been confided to them.

These courtiers were not the only enemies Magellan had to face. King Manuel, on hearing of the success of his discarded soldier, became very much excited, and resolved, if possible, to stop the expedition. He began to see that he had made a great blunder in treating Magellan so rudely, and in haughtily rejecting his offer of service; and feared lest, after all, the king of Spain should reap the benefits which he himself might have received, had he been less obdurate, from Magellan's zeal and genius.

At the Spanish court was a great Portuguese noble, named Alvaro da Costa, who was King Manuel's ambassador. To him King Manuel sent word to do everything in his power to prevent Magellan's expedition from setting out. Da Costa was very anxious to please his master, for he hoped for promotion if he served him well. He lost no time in undertaking the task now imposed upon him; and resolved that, at all hazards, Magellan should not sail, if he could possibly help it.

The first thing he did was to appeal to King Charles, and implore him to withdraw his promises. He told the king that if he allowed Magellan to go, he would mortally offend the Portuguese monarch. But this did not move King

Charles, who stood stoutly by his word to Magellan; and in this he was encouraged by the good bishop of Burgos, who was one of Magellan's warmest friends.

Failing to persuade the king, Da Costa next tried with all his might to prevail on Magellan himself to give up his expedition.

Magellan had now returned to Seville, where he was busy making his preparations for departure, and also for his marriage; for he was eager to make his dear Beatrix his wife, before he went.

One day, as he was absorbed in packing some baskets and boxes of provisions and clothing at his lodgings, he heard a loud knock at his door, and Sebastian Alvarez, King Manuel's agent in Seville, an old acquaintance of Magellan's, entered the room.

Magellan greeted him cordially, and asked him to be seated; whereupon Alvarez began to try to persuade him to give up his expedition.

"The road you are going on," he said, "has as many dangers as St. Catherine's wheel, and you ought to leave it, and take the straight road. In doing what you propose, you will mortally offend your liege lord, King Manuel, who will set you down as a traitor."

"Not justly," was Magellan's reply; "for I hope by my discoveries to shed lustre on our name, and do honor to the Portuguese crown. If I should go back to Portugal, there would be nothing left for me but the seven ells of serge, and the beads of acorns of a hermit."

"Nay, if you obey the king, he will do you honor; if not, you must suffer his vengeance."

But Magellan could not be dissuaded from his purpose; and Alvarez was forced to leave him in despair, and report his ill-success to King Manuel. Then da Costa, the ambassador, concocted still darker schemes against Magellan. Resolved to prevent his departure at all hazards, he plotted to have him killed. He secretly hired an assassin, who one night fell upon Magellan in one of the by-streets of Seville. But the young cavalier, though lame, proved more than a match for his dastardly assailant. As the latter was about to plunge a dagger in his breast, Magellan whirled around, drew his sword quick as a flash, and dealt the fellow a frightful blow across the face, and drove him, howling with pain, into the darkness.

An Attempt to Assassinate Magellan. Page 54.

Failing in this cowardly crime, da Costa sent his agents to Seville, to stir up the common people against his countryman. They went about among the inns and wine-shops, and told the Spaniards they were fools to submit to it that a foreigner should command a Spanish fleet; and so excited them, that one day, as Magellan was passing along the street, he was attacked by a furious mob. He made haste to enter the house of a friend, which fortunately stood near by, and thus escaped being pelted to death.

He was so happy just at this time, however, that these attempts upon his life were forgotten almost as soon as they were made; for the day rapidly approached when he would lead his fair Beatrix to the altar, and claim her forever as his own. The preparations for this event were carried forward in all haste; and for weeks the spacious mansion of Don Diego Barbosa, was full of bustle and excitement.

It was on a fresh, crisp winter's day that the bridal procession wended its way to the stately and beautiful cathedral of Seville. There was Magellan, attended by his own faithful friend, Faleiro, and a gay crowd of young nobles and soldiers; arrayed in his handsomest suit of velvet, silk and gold lace, and with a face beaming with proud pleasure. There was the bride, in her splendid wedding robe, surrounded by a sparkling bevy of dark Spanish beauties. There was the bluff old cavalier, Don Diego, in his official dress as mayor of the city, looking delighted and happy. And there, at the high altar, stood the bishop of Seville, in cope and mitre, ready to perform the solemn rites which should make the happy couple one.

The arches of the great cathedral resounded with the organ and the sacred chant; bride and bridegroom approached, and knelt at the altar; the momentous words were slowly spoken by the bishop; and then Magellan, with head erect, and a flush upon his cheek, advanced down the nave, with his blooming bride upon his arm. Alas! Neither knew how brief would be their married life, or that it would end with their happy honeymoon!

It was during this brief season of his honeymoon that Magellan tore himself away from the sweet companionship of Beatrix, to watch the preparations for his departure. One by one the good ships which were to sail under his command appeared in the harbor of Seville; one and all either newly built or newly repaired, with sturdy masts and unsoiled sails, and bedecked with fresh paint from stem to stern.

First, there was the "Trinidad," a small ship, indeed, compared with those which we see to-day, for it was only of one hundred tons burden, but in that time a good-sized craft, well able, it seemed, to breast the storms and wild winds of the Atlantic. This was the flag-ship, in which Magellan himself was to go.

Then there were the "San Antonio" and the "Conception," smaller vessels, of eighty tons burden each, commanded, the first by Juan de Cartagena, a Spanish captain with whom Magellan was destined later to have much trouble; and the other by Gaspar de Quesada. There were finally the "Victoria," and "Santiago," of sixty tons each, commanded by Luis de Mendoza and Juan Serrano, a relation of that friend of Magellan who had told him such exciting stories about the Molucca islands, which he was now going to try to find.

These ships were all quickly provided with

everything required for a long voyage. The "Trinidad" carried four large iron cannon; and in all, there were eighty cannon on the five vessels. Ample provisions were packed in the holds, and an abundance of such clothing as the officers and crews would need for an uncertain period, was supplied.

Inasmuch as Magellan was going among savage tribes, who were pleased with gewgaws and bright-colored clothing, a part of the cargoes of the ships was composed of copper, quicksilver, colored cloths, and handsome silks, jackets ornamented with copper and silver buttons, and a great variety of bells, bracelets, rings, and other trinkets.

Magellan, while thus supervising the preparations of his expedition, did not neglect one important task; that of studying the art of navigation. This was not, it is true, a wholly new study for him. His boyish fondness for ships and voyages had interested him in the art of managing vessels, and in the uses of the astrolabe and other nautical instruments. From the conversations he had had with Vasco da Gama, and other heroes of the ocean, he had derived much precious

knowledge ; and his voyage to India and back
had enabled him to observe closely the practical
working of a ship.

In the long winter evenings, when he had
returned from inspecting the progress made in
his fleet, you might have seen him seated before
a blazing fire in Don Diego's library—for Don
Diego was a man of learning, and had many valuable books, for which he had paid great prices—
with heavy tomes upon his knee, deep in their
contents ; or bending over a long table, where he
had spread out some rude chart of the Atlantic
or of the American coast, which had been drawn
by an earlier navigator.

By his side, deeply absorbed in his pursuit, sat
his fair young wife ; her face now sad with the
thought of separating from him ; now lit up
with tender pride, as she reflected what fame and
wealth his genius might win from the voyage.

Thus usefully and pleasantly were spent the
months that intervened between his marriage and
the time for him to set out on his daring venture.

At last that exciting moment came.   The
ships were all ready, moored side by side along
the quays of Seville. The sailors, some of whom

were Portuguese and some Spanish, were gathered in the city, and had, for the most part, taken up their quarters on board the vessels; and they were one and all impatient to sail. The captains and pilots were on board, as anxious as the sailors to depart.

It was on a soft August morning, in 1519, that Magellan rose, attired himself in his admiral's uniform, and lingered for awhile, locked in his wife's close embrace. He needed all his self-restraint to remain composed, and to utter every tender and consoling word that he could think of, to soften her sorrow at the parting. Then, gently withdrawing himself from her clinging arms, he gave her a last, long, loving look, and slowly passed into the street. There his attendants awaited him—his servants, and some of the sailors from the flag-ship. Don Diego was there, too, ready to accompany his son-in-law to the quays; and Don Diego's young son, Edward Barbosa, who was to go with Magellan and share his perils, was by his father's side. They mounted their horses and slowly rode through the streets.

Every thoroughfare was crowded. It was always a holiday with the gay and pleasure-loving Sevillians, when a great expedition was to set sail from their port on a voyage of discovery; and they had long known of Magellan's hardy project. There was now no trace of the miserable jealousy which had stirred a mob to assail him, but one and all, by their faces and cheers, seemed anxious to give him a hearty " God-speed."

Arrived at the quays, Magellan descended from his horse, embraced Don Diego and the other friends who had gathered to bid him adieu, and attended by Edward Barbosa, his officers and sailors, went on board the flag-ship and ascended to the deck. At the same time, the other captains appeared on their decks, and the crews began to weigh anchor and spread the white new sails.

It was a noble sight to see the five comely ships, almost side by side, slowly creep out of the lovely harbor; the sun flashing on the flags and pennons that floated from the masts, and making the new paint on the ships' sides glitter; a gentle breeze just ruffling the blue waves, and stirring them from a glassy calm; the quays alive with the chattering, noisy, and picturesquely attired crowd; the cannon pealing forth their deafening salvos from ship and shore; the captains erect on their decks, waving their plumed hats, and every now and then turning to shout their orders to their subalterns; and the lofty towers of cathedral and palace growing more and more dim and fairy-like as the little fleet floated away from the mole, and sped cheerily out upon the broad sweep of the river that flowed to the Atlantic!

Soon the eyes of the people on the quays were vainly strained seaward, and the eyes of those on the ships gazed without avail in the direction that the city stood.

Magellan was fairly off at last. What adventures would he meet with; what wonderful things would he discover on the surging deep?

CHAPTER V.

MAGELLAN CROSSES THE ATLANTIC.

OME time elapsed, after sailing from Seville, before Magellan put out into the open sea. After passing down the Guadalquivir, and narrowly escaping being stranded on two ruined pillars, which were in the bottom of the river, and had once supported a fine bridge built by the Moors, the ships reached the hoary old castle of St. Lucar, that lifted its towers high above the stream.

This castle belonged to the Duke of Medina Sidonia, one of the greatest nobles in Spain ; and just below it was a good port, at the mouth of the river, whence vessels could readily sail out upon the ocean.

Finding, when he reached this port, that the winds were contrary, and being in no hurry, Magellan anchored, and awaited more favorable breezes. The interval was employed in adding to the ships' stores some necessaries that had been overlooked, and in religious exercises. Magellan caused all his sailors to go ashore, attend mass, and make confession before their departure; and he himself set the example.

One day, Magellan summoned all his captains and officers on board the flag-ship, and told them the rules by which he wished the fleet to be guided.

"First," he said, " my flag-ship shall sail ahead, and the other ships follow; and that you may not lose sight of me at night, I will cause a burning torch to be set upon the poop-deck, which shall be kept burning as long as it is dark. When I wish to tack, the wind being contrary, or to make less way, I will show two lights. I have on board, you know, some torches made of reeds, well soaked in water, beaten flat, and dried in the sun; these will burn brightly. When I wish you to lower your small sail, I will burn three lights; and if I suddenly put out two of these, and leave a single light burning, you may know that you are to stop and turn. Should I espy any land or shoal ahead, I will cause a bombard to be fired off; and if I desire to make all sail, I will show four lights. Your answering signals will be similar lights, displayed in response to mine. As to watches, you will cause three to be kept at night; one at dusk, a second at midnight, and the third at break of day; and you must change the watches every night. Now, observe well these rules; that you may not forget them, here they are in writing, a copy for each of you."

At last, to Magellan's great relief, the wind shifted, and blew from the right quarter; and on the 20th of September, 1519, the little fleet set forth from the harbor of St. Lucar, and was soon buffeting the waves of the Atlantic.

Magellan directed his course northwesterly. He knew that in order to pass, as he felt confident it was possible for him to do, around the South American continent, he must steer more to the south than had the previous expeditions. Already a Spanish expedition had reached the fortieth degree of latitude south, on what is now the coast of Brazil; and thrilling news had come of Balboa's discovery of a farther Ocean. That a great ocean lay beyond the newly-found conti-tinent, was therefore certain ; and if that could be gained by doubling the land, there should be no doubt that the Molucca Islands, with all their bounteous wealth, could be reached ; and perhaps the globe itself might be encompassed by the doughty little fleet.

It did not take the ships long to reach the Canary Islands, grouped in the midst of the sea, off the African coast, and already occupied by lit-tle European settlements. They anchored at Teneriffe, one of these islands, and took in wood and water; and, soon after, stopped at another island, where they supplied themselves with an abundance of pitch.

On this island, Magellan was surprised to hear of a curious freak of nature, which, it was said, always took place there. He was told that every day at mid-day, a cloud came down from the sky, and enveloped a large tree; the rain fell from it on the leaves of this tree, and water was distilled from it, and formed a sort of fountain at the foot of the tree. This, he was assured, was the only supply of water that the inhabitants of the island, man or beast, had.

The fleet again set sail, and in no long time reached the Cape Verde Islands, not far from the Canaries, in a southwesterly direction. These were the last land that the adventurers were to stand upon until they sighted the long, dim coast of the New World; but so eager were one and all to strike across the ocean, and to see what was to be seen beyond, that Magellan made but a brief stay at the Cape Verdes. For some time they skirted the coast of Guinea, and saw the majestic group of the Sierra Leone in the hazy distance; and as they approached the equinoctial line, they began to be assailed by fierce gales and blinding rain-storms.

But they kept steadily on their way, Magellan's flag-ship, with its ever-glimmering lantern swinging on the poop-deck, and lighting up the billows, taking the lead; and at last found themselves quite out of sight of land.

As the ships rode through storm and sunshine, the voyagers observed many wonderful things, new to their astonished eyes. Often they were becalmed, and lazily floated hither and thither on the waves, waiting for the return of favorable breezes; and during these calms, they saw with amazement many monsters of the deep, of whose existence they had been utterly ignorant.

Sometimes great sharks, with long teeth and awful jaws, followed the ships for leagues and for days; and as soon as the sailors recovered from their surprise, they began to catch them—which was no difficult matter—with huge iron hooks, baited with pieces of colored cloth. When they had caught their first shark, they tried to eat him; but found his flesh anything but a savory morsel.

They saw, too, many curious birds, such as they had never before known of; and observed in one kind, that the females laid their eggs on the backs of the males. On one occasion, Magellan espied so large a number of flying fish, that they seemed to him to form an island in the sea.

Men in those days, even the wisest, were all superstitious, and believed in miracles, and strange appearances ; and on voyages, often imagined that they saw spirits, and were guided by spiritual agencies.

One dark night, when a storm of wind and rain was tossing the little fleet franctically to and fro, and rolling the waves high above the decks, and the sailors were moaning and praying, fearing that every instant would be their last, they thought that the spirit of Saint Anselm appeared to them, in the form of a dazzling light at the masthead; that he stayed there to comfort, and cheer, and give them courage, for several hours; and that when the spirit was about to depart, the light increased to such brilliancy as fairly to blind them.

No sooner had the spirit, as they believed it to be, departed, than the waves subsided, the wind fell to a gentle breeze, and the sea-birds began to gambol gaily among the sails.

It took Magellan and his companions a little more than two months to cross the Atlantic. Happily he had charts which enabled him to sail in the direction he desired, and which indicated the points at which he wished to arrive.

One morning in mid-December, the eyes of the voyagers were greeted with the sight of the long line of gray coast, which they had strained their eyes for many a day to espy. Thanks to Magellan's plan of showing lights, the ships had kept steadily together from first to last; and they now rode side-by-side, rapidly drawing near to the new continent.

When Magellan came near enough to distinguish the features of the coast, and the appearance of the country beyond, he looked about for a convenient harbor towards which to steer. It was fortunate that the coast itself did not present to his eye any very formidable difficulties; instead of being rocky and forbidding, it looked fair, sloping, and hospitable.

Running along about a league from the shore, parallel with it, he finally discovered a wide inlet, which seemed to be the mouth of a river. Here he resolved to put in; although, notwithstanding his charts, he was not quite certain where he was.

At first the region seemed to be deserted. The ships entered the wide inlet and anchored; and the sailors, crowding into the boats, pulled ashore, and leaped joyfully upon the strand. It was a hot day, but they were so glad to find themselves on land again, that they paid little attention to the burning rays of the sun, which blazed down on their heads from his zenith.

Then Magellan assembled all his officers and crews on the shore, and the priests, who were with them, set up a little altar on the beach. The men kneeled in a close body in front of the altars, the captains kneeling in front; and now, in this strange solitude, where all nature seemed to be in slumber, and where no vestige of any human habitation was yet visible, the solemn service of the mass was performed.

Magellan and his companions soon found that plenty of people dwelt on the shore they had reached, although these did not at first make their appearance. One of the pilots, named John Carvagio, had been in Brazil before, having gone with a previous expedition ; and he relieved the anxiety of his comrades by assuring them that the natives were peaceable and friendly, at least to Europeans, whom they regarded as superior beings.

It was not long before little groups of almost naked men and women began to make their appearance a little distance away, gazing curiously and timidly at the white men, and apparently afraid to approach nearer until they were reassured as to the intentions of the new-comers. The pilot Carvagio, who happily knew a few words of their language, at once went forward towards the nearest of these groups, and shouted out to them that they need fear nothing, for the Spaniards and Portuguese meant no harm, but were come as friends.

Upon this the natives drew nearer, and at last came up to the strangers, nodding and grinning, and chattering as fast as they could make their tongues go. At this moment, a warm, soft, pleasant rain began to fall, which was exceedingly welcome and refreshing on account of the heat.

No sooner had the savages perceived the rain, than they commenced playing all sorts of strange pranks, which filled the Europeans with astonishment. They capered wildly about, and lifted up their hands towards the clouds, holding their swarthy faces so that the drops should fall upon and run down them; sang a loud, discordant song, and finally, rushing forward, fell on their knees at the feet of the strangers, and began to repeat some words very fast, at the same time stretching their arms out, and clasping their hands.

Magellan asked the pilot what they meant by these capers; and Carvagio replied:

"They say that we have come from heaven,

bringing the blessed rain with us ; that it has been many weeks since it has rained in these parts, and that they worship us for causing it to fall."

It was fortunate that, at the beginning of their sojourn, the adventurers should have created so favorable an impression ; for now the natives set to work with a will, and built a long, low hut wherein their visitors might dwell and be sheltered as long as they remained. They brought them some pigs, which the sailors forthwith roasted and ate with great gusto. The pig's flesh was very re-freshing after the salt meat and hard-tack with which they had been forced to content them-selves during their long and weary voyage. The natives also laid before them some very curious bread, which proved, on being eaten, not nearly so nice as the pigs. It was made of the marrow of certain trees, and tasted something like very poor cheese.

Magellan found himself so hospitably treated on this coast, that he was in no great hurry to set sail again. The ships needed some repairs, and it was prudent to procure and store such provisions as could be found in the vicinity, and preserved for a voyage.

While the repairs were being made, and the
provisions stored, Magellan and his officers had
leisure to look around them. They observed the
natives with great curiosity. These lived in very
long, low huts, as many as a hundred, sometimes,
occupying a single hut. The natives did not
possess any iron implements, but built both their
houses and their boats with tools made of stones.
In their dwellings, which Magellan found himself quite free to enter whenever he pleased, he
saw that the beds were a sort of cotton hammocks, fastened to large timbers, and extending
across the wide room; and he was amused to
observe that the natives built their fires, to warm
themselves, directly under these hammocks.

Their boats they built all in one piece, out of
a single tree, and called them " canoes;" these
boats were large enough to hold thirty or forty
men, and were provided with oars shaped like
shovels.

As for the natives themselves, they were not
bad-looking people for savages. They were of a
brown color, with almost straight hair; many
of the women were almost fair, and quite
comely. The men did not wear any beards; for

these, it seemed, they were wont to pluck out, hair by hair. Both men and women went nearly naked, having for apparel only a belt made of parrot's feathers about their waists. It was a very common thing to see a man with three holes in his under lip, from which hung small round pebbles; and some of the women displayed the same strange ornament. Many of the natives, too, were branded in the face with curious figures, impressed in the flesh by means of fire.

When the men went to their work, their wives carried them luncheons in small baskets,which they poised on their heads; while in bags, fastened to their necks, they supported their babies. The men had, as weapons, long bows made of the black palm, and quivers full of arrows, made of cane, were hung across their shoulders.

One thing that surprised Magellan and his comrades, was the great number of parrots that were to be seen in that region. These were of all sizes, and their plumage was of the most variegated and gorgeous description. They also observed many small monkeys, yellow in color, and extremely amusing in their quick and lively ways; and there were also some strange-looking birds, which had beaks like a spoon, and no tongues.

As to the natural productions, they were very various and abundant. The fruit was large and luscious, and the grain rich and plentiful.

Magellan was sorry to make one discovery during his stay in this place, which greatly lessened his good opinion of the natives. On one occasion, after they had been having a fight with a neighboring tribe, they brought in several men and women, whom they had taken prisoners, and proceeded to kill them and cut them up. Soon after Magellan found these pieces of human flesh hung up at the chimney of one of the huts, and being dried by the fire. On asking what this meant, he was told that the pieces were dried to be eaten. He thus found that his savage friends were cannibals.

An amusing incident happened on the flag-ship, a few days before the departure of the fleet. The natives had become so familiar that they were in the habit of going freely on board the ships, and doing there pretty much as they liked. One day, a beautiful young girl, about seventeen, went on board the " Trinidad," and

was observed by Magellan to be peering cautiously about, and trying to escape being noticed.
Curious to know what she was about, he watched
her; and presently saw her creep up to a nail,
two or three inches long, that was driven into
the door of his cabin. She seized it, pulled it
out, and in a flash hid it in her long, abundant
hair. As she was without any other clothing
than the belt of parrot's feathers, her hair was her
only place of concealment. Magellan laughed
heartily to himself, and let her go away thinking
she had not been seen committing this little
theft. Her anxiety to possess herself of the nail
is explained by the great value the natives set on
iron, which seemed much more precious to them
than gold or silver.

CHAPTER VI.

THE MUTINY.

AVING taken a long rest from his Atlantic voyage, and provided his ships with all things necessary, Magellan again set sail, skirting the South American coast, and keeping a keen look-out for any inlet that might betoken a passage around the continent. He was resolved to search the coast narrowly, so that no such passage, if it existed, should escape him; and he therefore put in wherever a bay or river mouth appeared. After sailing for some days amid a warm and equable temperature, the fleet came to a wide inlet, which proved to be the mouth of a large river, some fifty miles wide where it entered the sea. This was what we now call the River de la Plata, upon whose banks stand, not far from the mouth, the flourishing cities of Buenos Ayres and Monte Video

The ships readily anchored in the river mouth, and once more the adventurers landed upon the unfamiliar coast. Scarcely had they done so, before they perceived that they were in the midst of a very different race from that they had encountered at their first landing-place. These savages were outright cannibals, and made daily meals upon their captured enemies. They were, moreover, exceedingly tall, strongly-built men, who seemed to the Spaniards no less than giants.

One of these men, evidently a chief, taller even than his companions, went fearlessly on board the flag-ship; but while he was there, the other natives took everything they could carry from their huts, and hurried away over the hills. Magellan ordered a hundred of his men to land and pursue them; but the natives were so agile, and took such enormous strides, that the pursuit was in vain.

On the pretty islands that studded the bay Magellan found some precious stones, which he took good care to store away, at the same time resolving on his return to search for more.

Setting sail again, the ships presently came to

two islands, just off the coast, where the crews went ashore, to procure some wild fowl which they saw on the strand. They were much astonished at some black geese they found, with beaks like crows, and which could not fly. They also succeeded in capturing many seals, which were not less strange to them, in color and shape, than the geese. During their stay at these islands, the ships were nearly destroyed by a mighty storm that swept over them; but they were stout and well-manned, and succeeded in weathering it.

After passing the Gulf of St. Mathias, and the bay of St. George, they reached a point which from the multitude of geese seen on the shore, Magellan named "Goose Harbor." Nowhere, as yet, had the gallant Admiral found a passage to the Pacific; but his courage and hopefulness were unabated, and he pressed vigorously on to the goal he was confident that, sooner or later, he should reach. He had now at least gone further south than any previous expedition had sailed; he was nearer the Antarctic pole than any European had been; and there was every reason for him to look forward cheerily to the accomplishment of the great end he had in view.

The southern winter, cold and blustering, had fairly set in, when one morning Magellan espied a large inviting bay, which seemed well sheltered from the bleak winds, and the shores of which had the appearance of affording a good supply of wood and water. Of these the ships were now sadly in want, for little had been found at Goose Harbor, their last stopping-place. Moreover, the ships needed many repairs; nor could Magellan hope to pursue his voyage successfully for some months to come. The crews were grumbling at hardships they were forced to suffer; and more than one of Magellan's captains betrayed open signs of discontent.

The admiral therefore deemed it best to put in at the pleasant-looking bay, and if it proved as comfortable as it looked, to stay there until fairer winds blew, and the return of spring brought a softer temperature.

The ships anchored in the bay, which Magellan, with the piety of his age and bringing-up, named St. Julian. It turned out an easy matter to land upon the sloping and still smiling shore, for winter was but fairly begun ; and the crews set to work to make themselves as snug as possible.

Scarcely, however, had the fleet reached what seemed so secure a haven for their winter sojourn when an event occurred which at first threatened, not only the success of the expedition, but the very lives of Magellan and his friends.

Of the captains commanding the ships in Magellan's fleet, three were Spaniards—Juan de Cartagena, Gaspar de Quesada, and Louis de Mendoza. Cartagena and Mendoza had been jealous, from the first, of the preference given by their king to Magellan, a Portuguese and a stranger, in putting him at the head of the expedition; and throughout the voyage had in various ways betrayed their ill-temper and discontent. Of the two, Juan de Cartagena, who was the second officer of the fleet, and commanded the " San Antonio," nourished the fiercest hatred of Magellan. He was a large, darkfeatured man, with a sour, malignant countenance, and he cherished the fixed idea that he, and not Magellan, should have been Admiral. From the first, he resolved on the earliest opportunity to

raise the standard of revolt. Finding that Mendoza shared his ill-will towards Magellan, and was
ready to enter into a plot against him, Cartagena
held frequent conferences with Mendoza, when
Magellan was engaged in other matters. While
scouring the country around St. Julian, in the early
days of their stay there, the treacherous captains
found many occasions to meet and mature their
project. They felt sure of being able to secure the
assistance of the sailors under their commands; for
most of these were Spaniards like themselves,
imbued with a fierce jealousy of the Portuguese; and besides, the sailors had become very
much discontented by their many hardships, and
by the long delays in the voyage.

It was not long before the plot was ripe for
execution. Cartagena and Mendoza revealed
it to the Spanish sailors on their ships, who
readily agreed to aid in carrying it out. The
first object was to secure Quesada, the captain of
the "Conception," who, though a Spaniard, was
suspected of being a staunch friend to Magellan.
His ship lay next to the "San Antonio," which
Cartagena commanded. Cartagena now resolved
to man one of his boats with twenty men, fully

armed, and to take advantage of a dark night to board the "Conception," seize Quesada, engage his sailors to take part in the mutiny, and with this accession of force to assault the flag-ship, the "Trinidad," itself. Magellan was then to be seized and killed on the spot; the other ship, the "Santiago," commanded by Magellan's cousin Serrano, was in like manner to be seized, and Cartagena would then assume command of the fleet.

One black night, therefore, Cartagena executed his project to seize Quesada. This he succeeded, with little difficulty, in doing; but before he could pursue his plan further, Magellan got wind of what was going on. Early the next morning, he sent a boat to the two revolted ships, with the message that they should be beached and careened. When the boat arrived alongside the "San Antonio," the sailors found the guns of the ship pointed at them; and one of the lieutenants shouted out harshly, and demanded to know what they wanted.

"The Admiral commands you to beach and careen your ship," was the reply. "We obey no orders," retorted the lieutenant, "but those of Juan de Cartagena, the true Admiral of the fleet."

The sailors rowed back in all haste to Magellan's ship. He now saw that there was open mutiny against him, and that it was necessary to take prompt and stern measures to repress it. Calling Fernandes, his chief constable, he told him to man the boat, proceed without delay to Mendoza's ship, and, if possible, take him prisoner. Six well-armed, stalwart men accompanied Fernandes on this hazardous venture. When the boat came alongside the " Victoria," Mendoza's ship, Fernandes called to Mendoza, and asked permission to board the ship. But this the captain refused to allow him to do.

"Surely," replied Fernandes, "you are not afraid of one man, bringing a letter to you."

Mendoza consulted a moment with his officers, and then bade Fernandes come on board.

No sooner had the constable leaped upon the deck, than he grasped Mendoza tightly in his arms, crying, "In the name of the king you are arrested!"

Before Mendoza's men could recover from their surprise, Fernandes's companions had rushed upon the deck with their swords drawn. They fell upon those who showed signs of resisting them; and soon several corpses lay weltering in their blood on the deck. In a few minutes, the brave fellows had subdued all resistance, and were in complete possession of the ship. Fernandes still held the unfortunate captain by the throat. Fiercely addressing him, at the same time shaking the breath out of him, the constable cried:

"You traitor, you shall die!"

Throwing Mendoza on the deck, he held him down with his knees, and drawing a huge dagger from his belt, plunged it deep into Mendoza's throat. The captain writhed in anguish, and in another moment lay stark dead upon his deck.

Magellan observed the success of Fernandes's stratagem from the deck of the flag-ship. He now ordered the " Trinidad" to drop down alongside the " Victoria;" he put his men under arms, and had his cannon loaded and aimed; and was soon able to pass from one deck to the other. He found that Fernandes and his men had already secured and bound the rebellious sailors; and having made a strict but rapid inquiry into the mutiny, he commanded six of the chief offenders to be brought out and hung, without mercy, at the yard-arms. Then he caused Mendoza's body to be hoisted by the feet on one of the masts, so that it might be distinctly seen by the crews on the other ships.

It remained to overcome the chief conspirator, who, with a strong force, held out on the "San Antonio." Magellan knew that he was still surrounded by Spaniards, who might be his enemies; and suspected that Cartagena's force might be too strong for him, if he assailed him directly. He therefore resorted to a shrewd stratagem.

Calling aside one of the sailors, upon whom, though he was a Spaniard, Magellan knew he could rely, he told him to take a boat, and row in all haste to the "San Antonio," as if he were escaping; and when he reached the ship, to beg to be taken on board as a fugitive.

The sailor promptly undertook the task; shot out from the "Victoria" in a skiff, and was soon seen by Magellan clambering up the side of the "San Antonio." When night came on, the sailor quietly cut the cables, so that the "San Antonio" drifted directly down upon the "Victoria." As soon as it floated alongside, Magellan, shouted out, "Treason, treason!" leaped on board with his men, fiercely attacked Cartagena and the mutineers, and in a short time had made prisoners of all who were not killed in the fray.

The crew thus quelled, Magellan hastened to set free Quesada and Mesquita, whom Cartagena had loaded with irons, and shut up in his hold. To his brother-in-law, Edward Barbosa, who had come with him, he confided the command of the "Victoria;" while he made his faithful friend, Mesquita, captain of the "San Antonio."

One ship, the "Conception," (the captain of which was Quesada), still remained in rebellion; but this, on seeing the others in the hands of Magellan, surrendered at discretion without a struggle. Thus the gallant Admiral, by boldly attacking his enemies as soon as he discovered their plot against him, achieved a prompt and complete victory.

Magellan was not naturally stern or relentless. He was never known to be guilty of an act of wanton cruelty. But he now saw that self-preservation, as well as the success of the expedition, demanded that his prisoners, especially the ringleaders in the mutiny, should be treated with the greatest severity. The punishment for mutiny in his days, as it is now, was death. To allow Cartagena and his confederates to live, would be to encourage a repetition of the revolt.

Calling the rebellious captain before him, therefore, on the deck of the "Victoria," Magellan coldly addressed him as follows:

"Juan de Cartagena, you have been guilty of an unpardonable crime. You have never had any provocation from me, to seek my life. My chief fault in your eyes is that I am a Portuguese, and not a Spaniard; but you well know that the sovereign of Spain hath entrusted me with the command of this fleet, and hath given me all power to direct its course. You have defied and rebelled against the king, in assuming to declare yourself its commander; and you have sought to gain this by bloodshed and murder. Cartagena, you deserve no pity. Prepare to die. You are to be shot and quartered, and your body shall be fixed to a stake, set up on this strange shore."

Cartagena hung his head in sullen silence, turning deadly pale, and clenching his hands, when his doom was pronounced. Magellan turned to two soldiers, and waved his hand. The miserable captain was seized and dragged to the forward part of the deck; and presently fell, shot through the heart.

Both his body and that of Mendoza were then quartered, and, as the admiral had directed, set upon stakes, on the shore.

The rest of the mutineers were kept in irons, except at such times as the ships needed pumping, when they were brought out, and, under guard, were set to the pumps.

Magellan, however, was not disposed to be too severe with the misguided wretches, who had been led into their crime by their captains. Soon after he released several of them, and put them on shore; telling them to explore the coast southward, to ascend any headland they might reach, and see if they could not espy the ocean on the other side. The mutineers, only too glad to recover their liberty, readily promised to obey his orders; and started off down the shore with brisk and lusty strides.

They remained away several days; and then returned, footsore and weary, to tell Magellan that they had not succeeded in making the desired discovery.

Order and submission were now restored throughout the fleet. The Spaniards, quite awed by the terrible fate of Cartagena and Mendoza, no longer thought of defying Magellan's authority; and the Portuguese ceased to harbor any ill-will against their mutinous comrades. Only one of the ships, the "Conception," was now under the command of a Spaniard; this was Quesada, whom Magellan fully trusted as his friend.

CHAPTER VII.

ADVENTURES WITH THE GIANTS.

HE adventurers were amazed that, as at their first landing-place on the South American coast, they did not see signs of any human beings or habitations at St. Julian.

The country round about seemed desolate and deserted. They began to think that it had no population whatever, but was abandoned to wild beasts and wild fowl. For two long months they searched the neighborhood in vain for some vestiges of human life; but none appeared.

At last, however, they were undeceived in this respect. One day, a gigantic figure suddenly appeared on a hill-top very near the bay; he was entirely naked, with short, bristling white hair, and a fierce, swarthy face.

As soon as this man saw the sailors staring at him in wonder, he began to leap wildly up and down, waving his arms about. and singing, or rather howling, some strange song in a stentorian voice. Every now and then he would bend down and grasp a handful of dirt, and sprinkle it on his great, bullet-shaped head, at the same time making a hideous grimace. Magellan was then sojourning on one of the islands that studded the bay. On being told of the strange apparition on the hill, he called one of the sailors, told him to go ashore and approach the big native, and to dance about and sing as he went up to him, so that the native might see that his intentions were friendly.

The sailor did as he was bidden. He went leaping and shouting up the hill, to the great amusement of his brother sailors, who were looking on. The native, too, gazed hard at him ; but soon recovering from his fright at seeing a white man drawing near, he strode towards the sailor, and began to caper around him. The sailor at last persuaded him to go in a boat to Magellan's quarters.

On coming into the Admiral's presence, and seeing so many strange faces and dresses about him, the gigantic savage grew timid ; and with

an expression of awe on his dark face, pointed to
the sky, to intimate that he thought the Spaniards had come from heaven.

Meanwhile, Magellan observed him with curious interest. He saw that the savage's cheeks
were painted with red hearts, and that around his
eyes were yellow circles. His hair, it appeared,
was painted white, and on his arm he carried a
a shaggy skin ; while in one hand was a heavy
bow, and some arrows, made of cane, feathered
at one end, and with points of black cut stones
at the other.

Magellan, anxious to make friends with the
natives in this lonely place, where he must yet
sojourn many weeks, regaled the giant with food
and drink; and when he had had his fill, Magellan caused a mirror to be brought and set before
him. As soon as the giant saw himself in the
glass, he gave a loud cry, and leaped back so
suddenly and with such force that he sent three
or four of the sailors sprawling on the ground.
He soon recovered from his fright, however, and
laughed with a deafening voice. He was as
pleased as a child with several trinkets which
Magellan offered him—two tinkling bells, which

he held close to his ear, a comb, which he very quickly saw how to use, and a chaplet of beads, which he tried to bite, making many grimaces, and then hung around his neck. Magellan then sent the giant ashore with four armed men; these the giant at once conducted to a group of his countrymen, who had gathered on the hill-top, and were one and all naked, and as tall as himself. They received the four Spainards with singing and jumping, meanwhile pointing to the heavens in the same manner as the first comer had done.

Pretty soon some of the native women made their appearance. They wore shaggy skins about their waists, and their faces, painted in many colors, were hideous. While not as tall as the men, they were much larger than European women.

The four Spaniards returned to the fleet, taking with them several of the chiefs, and recounting all that they had seen. Magellan gave the chiefs some bells, and some pictures painted on paper, which seemed greatly to delight them; for they began to sing in hoarse, loud voices, and to caper wildly about on the shore. Then suddenly

one of them, taking a long arrow from his belt,
thrust it far down his throat, and drawing it out
again, made a sign, as if to say, " Was not that a
wonderful feat ?"

So pleased were the chiefs with the strangers,
that they begged Magellan to send some of his
men back with them, that they might see their
habitations in the woods. Magellan readily consented to this, and ordered seven armed men to
accompany his sable guests back to the shore.

The chiefs led the way, and after crossing the
hills near the shore, plunged into a dense and track-
less forest, so tangled and overgrown that, though
the natives passed through nimbly enough, the
Spaniards were continually stumbling and falling
down. Meanwhile, they watched their guides
narrowly, ready to shoot them at the first sign
of perfidy.

After scrambling through the thicket for seven
miles, they came to an opening ; and here they
saw a long, low hut, roofed with the thick, shaggy
skins of wild beasts. This hut they found divided, by a curtain of skins, into two compart-
ments, one of which was occupied by the men,
and the other by the women and children. In all

there were thirteen women and children, and five men; and these eagerly welcomed the Spaniards, and regaled them with a roasted sheep, which they slaughtered for the purpose.

The Spaniards were persuaded to remain one night at the hut; and were offered a snug corner, with skins for coverings. The natives slept in the other corners; and so horribly did they snore, that their guests got but little sleep during the night.

The next day, the Spaniards invited the chiefs to return to the ships, with their families. At first they declined the invitation; but finally retired into the women's apartment, as if to bring them out to go. Presently they emerged again, their gigantic forms completely covered with heavy skins, their faces painted so as to give them a terrible aspect, and holding in their hands bows and a quantity of arrows.

Their appearance so terrified one of the Spaniards, that on the impulse of the moment he raised his gun and fired. To the astonishment of his companions, the report of the gun, instead of arousing the anger of the natives, made them tremble and lift up their arms, as if they imagined the noise to proceed from heaven. They were evidently persuaded of this, for they now very meekly followed the Spaniards towards the ships; but they did not allow their women to go. As they were passing through the forest, the natives were so much more fleet of foot that they soon outstripped the others, and all of a sudden, disappeared among the trees. The Spaniards searched for them in vain, and were finally obliged to return to the ships without them. On going with a strong force, a few days after, to the opening where the hut was, they found it quite deserted. The natives, with their families, had fled in all haste.

It was not long, however, before they had other visitors of gigantic stature and swarthy hue. One day, another big fellow, armed with bow and arrows, and painted as the rest had been, came up to some of the sailors, who were busily cutting wood on the shore. He approached them slowly, touching his head and breast with his fingers, and then pointing heavenward. He was a good-natured, smiling giant, and full of lively spirits; and was easily persuaded to accompany the sailors to Magellan.

The Admiral, pleased to see by this that the natives had not become hostile, cordially greeted him, gave him a cloth tunic, a pair of breeches, a cap, a comb, and some bells, and treated him to such food as there was at the camp. The native seemed very willing to remain with his new friends; and Magellan gave him a lodging in a hut on the island where he himself had his quarters.

After a time, the giant not only learned to speak Spanish very well, but was persuaded by one of the priests to become a Christian. He was baptized, and received the name of John. He often went ashore, and brought back animals, which served as excellent provisions for the Spaniards.

From this native, and others that he from time to time brought to the camp, Magellan learned a great deal about the tribes that inhabited the inland country. They had, it appeared, many strange customs. When one was sick, instead of taking medicine, he thrust an arrow down his throat; and this proved a very effectual emetic. When they were tortured with the headache, they cut themselves across the forehead, legs, and arms, which was their very simple way of bleeding themselves. They all wore their hair cropped close; and when they went hunting, they tied a cord around their heads, and upon this hung their arrows. They were a wandering people, living in one place but a short time, and then changing their abode. They lived, for the most part, on raw meat, and a sweet root which they called "capac." The sailors were amazed to see some of their swarthy guests skin rats and eat them raw; one of them would eat an enormous quantity of biscuits, and seemed to drink water by the quart. One striking thing about them was their exceeding swiftness of foot; and they seemed to run as rapidly in a dense, entangled forest, as upon the smooth, yielding sand of the seashore.

The idea occurred to Magellan that it might be useful to him in the future, if he could manage to keep one or two of these natives, and carry them with him on the rest of his voyage. They might act as interpreters with the savage races further south; and might point out the favorable places for anchorage, and the shoals and reefs to be avoided.

With this view he enticed two of the younger

and more comely and intelligent savages on board the flag-ship, and made them happy by profuse gifts. Among these were glittering steel knives, forks, small round mirrors, bells, and various articles of glass; which the big fellows received with the liveliest and roughest demonstrations of joy. Then he had some irons, with which captains were accustomed to confine rebellious sailors, brought out. These were shown to the natives, who examined them with the keenest curiosity. After they had played with them, Magellan showed them how to fasten the irons on their feet; but, no sooner had they found themselves securely bound about the ankles, than they fell in a great rage, and roared and foamed at the mouth like two bulls, and called upon their god, Setebos, to rescue them. They fell on the deck, and writhed about, as if trying to escape,

Meanwhile, some of the other natives, who had come with them on board, went ashore, and told the men and women what had happened; whereupon all the women made haste to run into the woods; while the men gathered on the shore, and began firing arrows at the flag-ship. One of the sailors fell mortally wounded. Magellan ordered his men to answer the attack with their guns; which so frightened the giants on shore, that they made all haste to follow their wives into the woods.

From this time, the Spaniards saw no more of this race of giants, for on scouring the country they could find no trace of them. So the sailors burned their huts, and brought such provisions as they found in them to the ships. The two natives who had been put in irons were carefully guarded; for Magellan had learned by this time how agile and cunning these gigantic fellows were; and was resolved to keep these two with him. After awhile, they seemed to become reconciled to their lot. They were brought on deck, and the sailors taught them a little Spanish; so that they were soon able to make themselves understood. When they had recovered from their anger and their fright, they became very merry and chatty, and apparently forgot all about their countrymen, and even their wives, whom, at first, they had bewailed very piteously. Each ate enough for two men, and drank astonishing quantities of water; and, on being provided with seamen's suits, they learned to prefer this costume to their original nakedness. Magellan was greatly pleased to see how quickly and readily they became reconciled to their lot.

Weeks and months glided quickly by in this pleasant bay of St. Julian. The weather was, at times, severe; and had the ships not found a very safe anchorage, under the lee of the islands that studded the bay, they would have been in serious peril from the terrible tempests of wind and hail that swept over them. In time, however, the bleak season gradually passed away; and nature began to put on the fresh, light-green tints of spring. As the vegetation gradually appeared and grew, Magellan saw that he was indeed in a lovely country, endowed with many natural beauties, prolific in fruits and vegetables, and blessed with a delightful temperature.

It was time, however, to think of resuming the voyage. There seemed no further obstacle to the progress southward of the ships. They had been fully repaired by the carpenters Magellan had taken care to bring with him; had been newly caulked, their sails patched and mended, the holds thoroughly scoured and cleaned, and all things about them set to rights. Provisions in abundance had been secured by the good-will of the natives, who had been very willing to exchange meat and other food, the products of the country, for the trinkets which Magellan freely lavished upon them. Good water, too, had been found in the near vicinity of the bay, so that everything seemed provided for a comfortable voyage further down the coast.

Before setting sail, however, Magellan deemed it wise that one of the ships should be sent forward, to explore the coast at a little distance southward; and accordingly told Serrano, who commanded the "Santiago," the smallest vessel of the fleet, to set sail on this errand. It happened that after Serrano got outside the bay, a current seized his ship, and swept it so rapidly forward that it could not be steered; and before he knew it, the "Santiago" grounded upon some rocks. There was not a moment to be lost. The ship was hopelessly wrecked, and all that the crew could to do was to save themselves, and such of the provisions as they could quickly lay their hands on. Fortunately the boats proved uninjured. They were launched without delay, and every man on board was rescued.

The boats made all haste to return to the fleet. The news of the loss of the "Santiago" was very unwelcome to Magellan ; for, though she was the smallest of his vessels, he could ill spare her from the fleet.

He resolved to delay no longer his departure from St. Julian. It was now late in August ; the time for a favorable voyage was fast gliding by, and there was no further reason for delay. One fine, warm morning, therefore, he gave his orders ; the "Trinidad," the Admiral's flag flying at her mast-head, floated smoothly out of the bay which had so well sheltered them, and where so many stirring events had taken place ; and the three remaining ships, with full sails on, followed closely in her wake.

CHAPTER VIII.

MAGELLAN DISCOVERS THE STRAITS.

T first the voyage southward was pursued under fair winds, and with soft breezes that wafted the ships swiftly over the waters. They had not proceeded for many days, when they came in sight of a promontory which jutted far out into the sea. Scarcely had they got opposite to it, when a terrific tempest burst upon them. The ships creaked, shook, and strained; some of the masts were carried away, and some of the sails were torn to shreds, as if ripped by unseen giant hands; and for several days it was an even chance whether the little fleet should founder or weather the storm. One of them came very near being dashed upon the grim and frowning promontory; another sprang a leak, and the men were forced to work desperately at the pumps night and day; a third narrowly

escaped being driven out to sea, and thus parting company with the rest.

At last, the fleet was able to find shelter below the promontory, in a little bay; and now
Magellan named the promontory Santa Cruz,
(or, the Promontory of the Holy Cross.)

Here the sailors once more grew clamorous to
return to Spain. They were worn and weary
with the voyage; they despaired of a successful
ending of the expedition; and they loudly demanded, even before the Admiral himself, that
the prows of the ships should be turned homeward.

But Magellan was not to be terrified into retreating. He sternly told his men to hold their
peace and trust in him.

"I shall go on," he said, "even till we reach
the ice-seas of the southern pole. The land of
this continent must end somewhere; and when
we reach this limit, we shall have achieved our
end. We have still food, water, and clothing,
and goodly ships. Why, then, should we despair?"

The confidence and courage of their commander restored the sailors to submission, and

they finally returned, without further complaint, to their tasks.

The voyagers only remained at Santa Cruz long enough to repair the damage which the storm had done to the fleet. Once more the flag-ship set forth, and the others followed, and favoring breezes carried them rapidly forward.

Magellan little thought, when he rose on the sunny morning of October 21st, 1520, that he was near the object most dear to his heart. It was the day consecrated to the eleven thousand virgins; and on all festival days of the Church, Magellan was wont to ordain a religious ceremony on the ships. On rising, therefore, he took care to attire himself in his finest suit, with velvet doublet, plumed cap, and jewelled sword; he little knew that he was habiting himself to witness the chief event of his life.

As he had proceeded along the coast, he had been blindly groping for a passage which he could only guess existed, but of which he had no positive knowledge whatever. He knew not what a day might bring forth; he was all in the dark as to the distance he had to go; and he had now become used to seeing the day go by, and the night

close in, without having made the great discovery.

When he emerged from his cabin, and stood
upon the deck, the officers and crews, in their
best apparel, were already assembled. Two
priests had set up a little altar on the poop, and
were standing, arrayed in their sacred robes,
ready to perform the mass. The Admiral took
his place in front of the rest; and as the good
ship sped on, the voices of the priests mingled
with the splash of the waters and the flapping of
the sails, in the performance of their solemn rite.

Scarcely was mass concluded, when one of the
sailors, perched on the look-out forward, cried out
loudly that a long cape was in sight. Magellan
walked to the side of the ship, and gazed in the
direction in which the sailor pointed. There, indeed, was a jutting cape, beyond which nothing
could be seen.

Pretty soon the fleet was off the point. On
rounding it, Magellan's heart leaped within him
to perceive that there was a broad inlet, running
in a southwesterly direction; and that, while the
land was plainly visible on its southern side, its
limit inland could not be discerned. Naming

the cape the Cape of Virgins, he gave orders that the fleet should boldly enter the inlet, and endeavor to find out whither it led.

The aspect of the shores, and of the inlet itself, was very remarkable. Lofty mountains, snow-shrouded, loomed on both shores. These shores were jagged and uneven, many lesser inlets running from the larger one far into the land, and craggy islands seeming in several places, to completely choke up the channel; here and there were patches of green forests, but the general appearance of the place was desolate and forbidding.

The ships advanced carefully, for on every side the jutting reefs and piled-up breakers threatened destruction. As the flag-ship progressed, Magellan anxiously watched the channel ahead, fearing every moment lest it should come to an end, and once more dash his hopes of a passage. At last they came to a round bay, sheltered on every side by lofty masses of rock. It was now nearly dark; the fleet could not pursue its course much further, amid so many perils; and Magellan gave the order to anchor in the bay.

So favorable for a sojourning place and point of departure did this bay appear to Magellan, when he rose next morning, that he resolved to remain in it, with the flag-ship, while he sent two of the other ships to explore the channel further on, and see if they could not find the outlet. Accordingly, calling Mesquita and Serrano, the captains of the "San Antonio," and the "Conception," he told them to set out, without delay, on this dangerous and difficult errand.

They had scarcely disappeared among the islands, before a storm arose, so fierce that the two ships that remained in the bay were forced to weigh their anchors, and be tossed to and fro violently at the will of the winds. This continued all night, and for the greater part of the next day; when at last the tempest subsided, without having seriously damaged the ships.

Meanwhile, no signs appeared of the two vessels that had gone forward to explore the channel; and for a time Magellan much feared that they had foundered in the storm. After several days, however, he was relieved by seeing them speeding rapidly towards the bay, and what filled his heart with good cheer, with their flags and streamers flying gaily from their mast-heads. They were soon alongside the flag-ship; and Mesquita, hastening on board, eagerly advanced to Magellan, and fell at his feet.

"Praise be to God, admiral," cried he, when he could recover his breath so as to speak, "we have found the outlet!"

Magellan, with flushed face, his whole body trembling with excitement and emotion, raised the faithful captain from the deck, and clasping him about the neck, burst into tears of joy.

"Is it indeed true?" he said, with faltering voice. "And have you seen the other ocean— the western ocean beyond?"

"We have indeed seen it, with these very eyes," replied Mesquita. "We came near perishing in the storm; but we kept on, and we have succeeded."

Magellan turned to Serrano, who had now come on board from the "Conception," and the other officers, and tenderly embraced them. Then in exultant tones, he spoke.

"My comrades, at last we have triumphed! Our perils have been great, our trials and hardships sore and many. But the reward of all has

come. The passage that conducts from the Atlantic to the further ocean, that affords the nearest way from Spain to the precious isles of the
Moluccas, is found! It is just before us; we
shall pass through it, if God pleases to still protect us, and shall sail into the ocean beyond. We
shall make other discoveries; find wealth and
fame for ourselves, and dominion for our monarch! Captains, repair to your ships; assemble
your crews, and tell them the good tidings; let
your cannon awake deafening echoes among
these crags; float the royal standard and ensigns
of Spain from your mast-heads; array your decks
with streamers and ribbons; let wine and meat
in plenty be set forth ; and render thanks to
God for conducting us to this great discovery!"

The admiral's orders were obeyed with a will.
Ere long the four ships, riding at anchor in the
bay, side-by-side, put on an air of festivity and
good cheer. The sailors crowded the decks,
singing and capering, embracing each other, and
every now and then breaking out into hoarse and
lusty cheers. The cannon boomed with quick
succeeding volleys, their voices of thunder re-
sounding from point to point; the flags waved

with joyous fluttering in the fresh breeze; and then followed a bounteous feast on each deck, of which officers and men partook together.

The religious thanksgiving for the discovery was not forgotten. The remains of the feast were cleaned away; instead of the tables, altars arose on the decks; and the priests, with deep-toned voices, chanted the song of triumph which their church ordained.

When he had grown somewhat calmer, Magellan took the two captains, Mesquita and Serrano, into his cabin, and asked them to relate the particulars of their adventures.

"At first," said Mesquita, "we met with head-winds, which would not allow us to weather the cape at the end of the bay; and we attempted to turn round, and come back to the other ships. In making this attempt, we were very near being stranded upon the shore. Every moment we feared that we should be lost; meanwhile, the tempest carried us gradually toward the head of the cape, which we finally reached. It seemed to us that the inlet ended there; and on rounding the cape, we were surprised to see a small mouth, or corner of the inlet. We sailed for this, in the hope of sheltering ourselves from the storm. On approaching nearer, we found that this led into another bay, which we forthwith entered. Crossing this bay we reached another narrow channel, through which we sailed, until we came to still a third bay, larger than either of the others; thence we passed into a third strait, from which we could plainly discover the boundless ocean itself. Lying there over-night, we returned to-day, to impart to you and our comrades the glorious news we brought."

The weather was fair, and seemed settled; and Magellan was eager to follow in the route that the "Conception" and the "San Antonio" had pursued. He therefore ordered the whole fleet to set sail, and advance through the channel. In no long time the ships had entered the last strait described by Mesquita; and all the adventurers now caught a glimpse, in the far and dim distance, of the white-crested billows of the further ocean. They then anchored off a cape that jutted into the strait, which Magellan named Cape Forward.

But Magellan found that, once here, he had by no means found an easy passage through. The channel seemed to divide into two, and to present two branches, one to the southeast, the other to the southwest. Which should be taken? Without doubt, one of them led to the ocean; the other probably found its termination in a bay; nor could he decide, from the point where he then was, which to attempt.

He therefore resolved to again send out the two ships, the "Conception" and the "San Antonio," to explore the two channels, and to report to him their discoveries. Before doing so, however, Magellan called together his officers and principal men, and said to them:

"We have, no doubt, discovered the passage from the Atlantic to the further seas. Ere very long our ships will ride the waters of the sea beyond. It remains to decide whether we shall push further forward, and seek the Moluccas; or return with our good news to Spain. We have only provisions for three months; the voyage to the islands must be very long and tedious; we may have to undergo stern trials, severe privations. On the other hand, if we succeed in reaching the Moluccas, vast riches await us there. We shall gain dominion for the king, and receive yet greater fame and honor in Spain, when at last we seek the hospitable shores of home. I ask you, comrades, for your voices. Which shall we do?"

A loud shout promptly answered the Admiral's question.

"Let us go on!" was the eager response of Magellan's companions.

One, however, Gomez, the pilot of the "San Antonio," did not join in the cry. When silence was restored, he spoke boldly in favor of returning to Spain.

"Our fleet," he said, "is worn with so much sailing. The ships are out of repair, and little able to withstand the storms of unknown seas. We have already lost one of them by shipwreck. Let us go back, and return next year with a new and larger fleet."

"Enough of this!" retorted Magellan, angrily. "We will go on, even if we have to eat the leather off the ship's yards!"

The "Conception" and the "San Antonio" started off on their errand of exploration; several days elapsed, but they did not return. Magellan feared that they were lost. He was too impatient to wait for them, however, and one day he set sail, with the two ships that remained, through the strait that led southwestward. This, on reflection, seemed most likely to lead to the open sea.

On their way they passed through a wide river, which, from the number of little fishes they found in it, Magellan named the River of Sardines. Anchoring in this river, he sent out two of the long-boats, well supplied with men and provisions, to reconnoitre the further end of the river. The boats returned after three days, with the intelligence that the river led to the sea, the shores of which they had touched.

As the "Trinidad" (the flag-ship) and the "Victoria" were advancing through the river, to Magellan's delight the "Conception," which he had given up for lost, suddenly appeared in view. She soon came alongside, and Serrano, the captain, told Magellan that he had got lost in the straits and among the islands. He had seen nothing of the "San Antonio" since he parted from her. Magellan accordingly sent back the "Victoria" to the entrance of the passage in search of her; and told the captain, if he did not find the missing vessel, to hoist a flag on the summit of a hill, and place a letter in a jar at the foot of the flag-pole; so that if the "San Antonio" saw the flag, its officers might learn by the letter, what course the fleet was holding.

The "Victoria" returned to the entrance, but saw no sign of the "San Antonio." The captain raised the flag, and deposited the letter, as he had been directed; and placed another flag and letter on a little island at the mouth of the strait.

What had really become of the "San Antonio," may be related here. The pilot, Gomez, who had urged Magellan to return to Spain, was indignant at the stern response he had received. He was one of those Spaniards who had all along been jealous of the Admiral; and, as it happened, most of the sailors who went in the "San Antonio" had the same vindictive feeling.

When, therefore, the "San Antonio" had got well out of sight of the fleet, and night had come on, Gomez incited the crew to mutiny. They seized Mesquita, the captain, Magellan's faithful friend, wounded him, put him in irons, and imprisoned him in his cabin. Then Gomez took command of the ship, sailed back through the strait, and at once put to sea on his way to Spain. On his arrival there, he everywhere spread the report that Magellan's expedition had miserably failed, and that the other ships had been lost; and this was believed there for many months.

The three other ships, the "Trinidad," "Conception," and "Victoria," soon reached the mouth of the River of Sardines. At the point where it flowed into the ocean appeared a hilly cape, stretching out into the water. This Magellan called Cape Desire, because, he said, this was a place he had long desired. As he saw beyond the jutting cliffs, the long sweep of billows, the boundless expanse of waters, his eyes filled with tears of joy, and he lifted his hands heavenward in mute thanksgiving to God, that at last his eyes were permitted to behold the ocean he had sought. Once more the cannon awoke the echoes of the lofty and forbidding shores, and once more the priests chanted their praises to the beneficent Creator.

Near Cape Desire the ships found a good harbor, where they could easily cast anchor, and where the crews could go ashore. On the high hills which, in this place, rose for a long distance from near the water's edge, and which terminated in towering, snow-crested mountains, they formed vast cedar forests, and plenty of pure spring water. They caught many fish, too, among them a fish that so much resembled sardines that they called them by that name ; and they found a sweet and succulent herb, which was similar to celery in taste and appearance. This grew in damp places, near the springs.

The prospect in every direction was very striking and picturesque. The crags and foaming gulfs of the straits, the lofty mountains, the rich green forests of cedar, the luxuriant herbage, and the limitless ocean, formed a scene which deeply impressed itself on the minds of the weary wanderers.

The adventurers greatly enjoyed their stay at Cape Desire. Their trials were forgotten amid the attractions of their resting place ; the weather was growing cooler, but was not yet bleak ; sea and land afforded an abundance of fresh provisions ; and the Admiral allowed his crews, while on shore, the largest liberty. They wandered among the odorous forests, and roamed over the hills, and some even ventured to climb one of the mountains, until they found themselves up to the waist in snow.

The natives of the region were very much like those whom they had seen on the other side of the straits; only they seemed brighter and more intelligent, and had a language which they spoke rapidly, with a guttural accent that amused the sailors very much. The latter soon learned enough of this strange jargon to talk a little with the natives, who, after they once became accustomed to the Europeans (the like of whom they had never before seen), were very good-natured and sociable. They were of gigantic stature, and made their faces hideous, by painting and branding them. They brought provisions to the ships, and were greatly delighted with the beads, buttons, little bells, and so on, with which Magellan rewarded them.

These natives lived for the most part on a juicy root which grew in great abundance in the marshy places, and which they cooked after a rude fashion. They had a way of rubbing sticks together very rapidly, with the pith of a tree between, and thus striking a light.

Magellan only tarried in this harbor long enough to repair his ships, rest his crews, and take in a fresh supply of wood, water, and provisions, and determine on his future course. He made an excursion along the coast, and perceived that, as far as he went, it stretched away almost due northward. He therefore concluded that, if he sailed in that direction, he would sooner or later reach the equator; and that, if on approaching this line, he altered his course towards the north-westward, he must in time arrive at the Moluccas. He had now constructed, in a rude way, a pretty fair chart of the world; though, of course, he could not give a true outline of the shape of the continents of Africa and South America.

One day, early in December, the fleet once more set forth, upon an ocean which, in that region at least, had never before been plowed by the keels of an European ship. More than a year had passed since the voyagers had sailed out of the harbor of Seville. What strange countries and peoples they had seen; what thrilling adventures they had had! But the perils and the scenes they had passed through were to be outdone by those they were yet destined to encounter.

CHAPTER IX.

CROSSING THE PACIFIC.

AIR and calm were the days, and smooth and sparkling was the sea, during the first weeks of Magellan's progress over the ocean, hitherto untraversed by European prows. The weather preserved an even temperature and tranquillity, which made the voyage seem more like a pleasure excursion than what it really was—a desperate and daring venture. The crews worked at their tasks with cheery good will; the ships sped on side-by-side; favorable breezes wafted them rapidly forward. It did not seem possible that aught could happen to disturb this prosperous setting-out.

Magellan, who was a good scholar, as well as a brave soldier and bold voyager, spent the long, sunshiny days poring over his charts, making calculations, and estimating the time it would take, if all went well, to reach the Moluccas. In the midst of these studies, a thrilling thought, one day, made him start to his feet, and clasp his hands. He was approaching the Moluccas by a westward route from Europe. But the islands had already been reached by an eastward route, around the Cape of Good Hope. If, then, after arriving at the Moluccas, he should, instead of re-tracing his voyage around South America, keep right on, double Africa, and thus get back to Spain, he would have circumnavigated the globe. No voyager had ever achieved this triumph; he would be the first to have encircled the earth!

He resolved on the spot, that he would add this new laurel to the crown of his fame. Alas! Though his glorious dream was realized, he was not destined to live to see it.

So tranquil did the waters of the ocean re-main, from day to day, and from week to week, that Magellan, impressed by this striking con-trast with the stormy and tempest-tossed Atlan-tic, resolved to bestow upon it a name suggestive of its serenity.

Calling his officers about him, one day, he thus spoke to them.

"My comrades, we are sailing on an unknown ocean. No European ship has ever before ploughed these gentle waters. On our charts, this vast expanse is nameless. Do you not see how smooth as a lake is its surface; how mild are its breezes; how soft and even is its temperature? Comrades, I will give this great sea a name, and christen it. Henceforth, let it be known as the PACIFIC!"

And so Magellan gave a name, not only to the stormy straits which he had discovered, but also to the mighty ocean which he was the first European voyager to cross.

After sailing for some weeks, the fleet was becalmed in mid-ocean. The winds which had sped the ships so buoyantly, fell, then died away. There was nothing to be done except to toss about on the lonely sea, and await the return of easterly breezes. But days, then weeks passed, and the dreary calm continued. Sometimes a brisk wind would come up, and the ships would then plough rapidly through the waves; but it would vanish again, and leave them once more idly floating.

At first, Magellan thought little of this. He

was annoyed not to make greater speed ; but there was plenty of time, he thought, before them. As weeks elapsed, however, the calms threatened evils to the adventurers far more serious than mere delay. On examining his supplies of provisions, Magellan perceived, to his dismay, that they were fast running short.

Long before this, he had hoped to come upon islands where his supplies could be replenished ; but day after day the same dreary expanse of waters, unbroken by so much as a speck of dry land, greeted his eyes. At last, however, an island did appear in sight. Magellan eagerly ordered the ships to make for it. They approached, only to find a heap of barren rocks, with a few stunted trees, and uninhabited, except by noisy sea-birds. Not even was there good anchorage ; while all about the ships swam hideous swarms of sharks, ready to seize, in their vast and gaping jaws, any luckless sailor who fell into the water, or even exposed himself in a boat.

Magellan was forced to sail away from the island without adding a fish or an herb to his provisions. Another month passed, amid provoking calms, and out of sight of land; then another island came in sight. This, too, proved bitterly disappointing; for there was little vegetation, and not a living thing appeared on its dismal and desolate surface. Here, however, some of the sailors managed to land, and succeeded in catching a few fish, which served to postpone, for a time at least, the approach of actual hunger.

The fleet had now crossed the tropic of Capricorn, and was rapidly nearing the equator. The heat grew intense. The sun blazed remorselessly down upon the tar who ventured up the masts. Men fell fainting and sun-stricken to the deck. The platform actually burned under their feet; the pitch which filled the seams softened and melted, and oozed out.

What made the heat still more unendurable, the supply of fresh water was now almost exhausted; what remained had become so filthy and nauseous that the wanderers could not drink it without shuddering, and it often made them ill.

Then Magellan was grief-stricken to be forced to reduce the rations of his brave and suffering comrades. The only food left consisted of coarse biscuit; and these were, as one who was on board says, "reduced to powder, and full of worms." They had been gnawed and defiled by rats, and were scarcely eatable. But even such food was a rich and rare luxury compared to that to which the poor fellows were at last reduced. In no long time not a biscuit, not a crumb remained. Then they were obliged to do the very thing that Magellan had spoken. of, when he said he would go forward, "even if they had to eat the leather off the yards." This miserable apology for food was now, indeed, all that was left. The gaunt and famished sailors tore off the ox-hides under the main yard, which had been placed there to protect the rigging from the strain of the yard. The leather was so tough that the hungry teeth could make no impression upon it. They attached pieces of it to strong cords, and let them trail in the sea for four or five days. When they were thus soaked through, the sailors made a poor pretence of cooking the leather. They placed it over the fire, until it was singed, and then ate it greedily.

When the leather was gone, they devoured

saw-dust, and eagerly hunted down the very rats that infested the ships, and when they caught one, quarrelled fiercely to secure a bit of him.

It seemed as if no misfortune were to be spared the unhappy voyagers; for, while they were suffering all the horrors of famine, that terrible sea distemper, the scurvy, broke out in their midst. The gums of its victims swelled, so that they could not eat even the wretched food still within their reach; and twenty of the sailors soon died of actual starvation. Others grew ill, and ere long there were scarcely enough to sail the ships.

An end came, however, to these terrible hardships at last. The fleet had sailed from Cape Desire early in December. In the first days of March, it came in sight of some islands, that rose green and blooming from the bosom of the sea, and even in the distance gave such promise of relief that the adventurers fell on their knees on deck, and fairly wept for joy.

There were three of the islands; one was larger than the others, and rose in wooded hills to quite a height. Towards this Magellan directed his course. When the ships approached to within a mile of it, of a sudden the water was

covered with long, slender boats, with three-cor.
nered sails, filled with a multitude of fantastic
figures. The canoes came swarming towards the
ships, their occupants crying out and making all
sorts of uncouth noises, and seeming to be not
in the least afraid of the strangers. It delighted
Magellan and his famished comrades to perceive
that they brought with them an abundance of
provisions. The natives went on board the ships
as boldly as if they were in the habit of seeing
Europeans every day; bringing in their arms
banana stalks hung thick with the luscious fruit,
cocoanuts, and other products of their island;
and pretty soon the voyagers were devouring
these good things with greedy eagerness.

The natives were really fine-looking men, with
smooth, olive skins, handsome and pleasant faces,
and tall, well-built forms. Many were quite
naked; some, however, wore girdles, or matted
aprons about the waist, and queer-looking hats,
made of palm leaves. A few wore beards, and
the thick hair fell, in some cases, down to the
waist.

Magellan and his officers treated their visitors
with grateful good will, and allowed them to

roam freely about the ships, which they seemed anxious to do; and ere long the vessels fairly swarmed with them in every part. They seemed perfectly harmless and good-natured, and danced and capered about wildly, when Magellan gave them some buttons and bells.

As he was standing on the deck, watching their pranks with an amused smile, one of the sailors came to him and said that the islanders had cunningly stolen the skiff, which had been fastened to the stern of the "Trinidad." Looking over the side, Magellan saw them making off with it. At the same moment, other sailors came up, and reported that the natives were laying hold of everything in the ships to which they took a fancy, and were carrying what they thus appropriated to their boats.

Magellan then ordered that they should be driven off the ships; which was at once done. This evidently enraged the savages very much; for no sooner had they got into their boats than they began pelting the Spaniards with stones and burning torches. Magellan then caused the cannon to be fired over their heads. This, at first, produced the desired result. The boats fled, amid much shrieking and yelling, to the island. In the night, however, they returned, and did much damage to the ships with their rude missiles.

The next morning Magellan, indignant at the thieving propensities of the natives, and resolved to recover the skiff they had stolen—for he could ill spare even a small boat—manned several boats with forty men, armed to the teeth, and taking his place in the foremost, went ashore. He found the island a lovely one, overgrown with luxuriant tropical fruits and plants, and adorned with beautiful forests. Proceeding inland from the shore, he soon came to a native village, from whence the inhabitants, seeing him approach, fled in dismay. He burned the greater part of the village, killed several of the natives, and took others prisoners; and then returned to the shore, where he found his skiff, with many canoes, moored in an inlet out of view of the ships.

Among his prisoners were a number of the native women. These, Magellan observed with curiosity and interest, were pretty and delicate, much fairer than the men, with loose and flowing raven tresses, which fell to the very ground.

They had no clothing, except aprons made of a thin and pliable bark; while their hair and faces were perfumed with cocoa oil. Magellan learned a great deal that was singular about the people and the island, from one of his male prisoners, who was very quick-witted, and who conversed with him by signs. It appeared that they subsisted chiefly on figs, sweet canes, birds, and fish. Both men and women were very fond of fishing in the sea, which was, indeed, their chief pastime; their fish-hooks were made of fish-bones. While the men worked in the fields, the women stayed at home in their huts, and made clothing and baskets of palm-leaves. The huts were built of wood, and thatched with fig-leaves; their beds had palm-leaf mats for covering, instead of blankets and quilts; the beds themselves being simply bundles of soft, fine palm straw. As for weapons, they used long sticks, with sharpened and pointed fish-bones at the end. The boats which Magellan found in the cove struck him as very odd. They were long, narrow affairs, painted red, black, or white. The masts consisted of crooked poles, which supported palm-leaf sails, shaped like lateen sails, both fore and aft. For paddles they had devices that looked like shovels.

Magellan remained off these islands three days. He gave them the name of the " Isles of Thieves," because of the depredations of the natives; and the islands are known by that name to this day.

On weighing anchor, and proceeding on its way westward, the fleet was followed by great crowds of the natives, in innumerable boats, who chaffed the Spaniards by holding fish up to them, as if to taunt them with their hunger. Then they would throw showers of stones, most of which, however, fell harmlessly into the water, short of the ships. They rowed so swiftly and skilfully that it was impossible to hit their boats with the cannon balls; nor did they desist and return to their islands until the fleet was far out to sea.

Magellan had now reached the eastern edge of that vast cluster of islands which comprises the Asiatic archipelago. He soon found himself constantly passing among groups of them ; but, as he had taken care to replenish his store of provisions and water before sailing from the Isles of Thieves, and was uncertain what his reception might be, he did not care to cast anchor among them. In ten days he found the islands becoming more dense, larger, and more luxurious in vegetation; and now he came to one that seemed so inviting, that he could not resist the temptation to land. The group of islands among which he was then passing he named the St. Lazarus Islands, because it was on the day of that saint that he reached them; but they are now known as the Philippine Islands. The island at which Magellan cast anchor and went ashore proved to be uninhabited; and he was not sorry for this, as he might land in peace, and rest his crews. He caused two large tents to be set upon the smooth beach, and the sick sailors were taken out of the ships and carried into them. There they were carefully tended, and most of them, in the balmy air, and supplied with good food, soon recovered their customary vigor. On this island, too, Magellan found plenty of pure water, which had long been one of his direst needs.

Not far from this island was a larger one which is now called Samar. Magellan had not been at anchor more than two days, when one

Meeting with the Natives. — Page 137.

of the sailors espied a long canoe, which was
rapidly approaching the shore where the Spaniards were. Magellan, with some of his officers,
walked boldly down to the beach, as if to meet the
new comers; at the same time cautioning his
men not to move or speak without his permission.

The natives sprang fearlessly upon the beach,
and went directly towards Magellan, whom they
appeared to recognize at once as the chief officer
of the fleet. As they came, they capered and
danced about, and grinned with their big mouths,
showing rows of dazzling white teeth, as a token
of friendly welcome. Magellan made signs to
them that he was glad to see them; whereupon,
a number ran along the beach, calling out to some
of their countrymen, who now appeared off the
island in canoes, and were fishing, to come on
shore.

It was a strange scene, this meeting of Asiatic
savages, creamy in color, completely naked, were
it not for the aprons of barks about their waists,
with great masses of shaggy hair, with the
Europeans, the chief of whom were as elegantly
attired as if they were on the point of attending

a royal court; the savages huddled together on one side, gazing curiously, and every now and then jumping up, and uttering hoarse exclamations; and the Europeans standing in a silent and attentive group, not forgetting to keep their hands on their weapons in case of a sudden attack.

But the natives evidently had no hostile purpose in their thoughts. They brought some just-caught and still wriggling fish, and laid them, with many signs of respect, at Magellan's feet. He was not less generous in his turn. Sending into the tents for some trinkets, he might soon have been seen, in the very midst of the natives, scattering among them a number of articles that fairly set them wild with delight. There were looking-glasses and combs, red caps and bells, toys of ivory, and gewgaws of silverware and brass. The natives were not content with lavishing fish upon the strangers. One of their canoes pushed off, and in a flash had disappeared; ere long, it was seen returning as rapidly as it went. Its occupants sprang ashore, bringing with them a huge jar. Placing this before Magellan, they produced cups made of cocoanut shells, dipped into the jar, and brought forth the cups overflowing with some kind of liquor. Magellan tasted it, and turning around, smiled and nodded his head, as if to say, "It is very nice." But this was only put on to please his visitors; it was really very unpleasant stuff, a sort of wine made of palms. The natives drank it with great gusto. Magellan liked much better the enormous figs they brought him, which were sweet and juicy; and the rich milk of the cocoanuts, which they cracked for his delectation.

The natives, indeed, proved so friendly, that Magellan not only secured from them what provisions he needed, with which to replenish his stores, but learned a great deal about that part of the great ocean where he now found himself. He was told that there were many larger islands ahead, all of which were inhabited by tribes with various traits and customs, and were very rich in their productions. He could not doubt that he was very near the far-famed Molucca Islands, so much coveted both by his adopted country, Spain, and his native country, Portugal. It seemed certain to him that the vast Continent of Asia lay not far to the North of him; those mysterious regions once comprising the dominions of the great Kubla Khan; and that, by sailing steadily westward, he should reach the shores of Africa, and find the kingdoms which Vasco da Gama had visited.

He found that he could trust his swarthy visitors; and no longer hesitated to take them on board the ships, and show them his cargo of spices and gold, his cabins, and his armament. On one occasion, he caused one of the cannon on board the "Trinidad" to be fired; which so much frightened the natives, that several of them sprang overboard into the sea, and were with difficulty rescued.

At last, the chief of the island from whence the natives came, himself paid a visit to the ships in state. He was attended by many nobles, and had his face painted; while heavy gold ear-rings hung from his ears, and gold bracelets encircled his wrists. He was an old man, with gentle manners, and a pleasant smile. With him he brought two boats laden with oranges, palm wine, and—what very much pleased Magellan— some chickens.

Before sailing away from the place where he

had met so pleasant a reception, Magellan visited several neighboring islands, in each of which he was welcomed in a most peaceful and friendly manner. On one of these he found people very different from those he had seen at first. They were of a tawny complexion, and very fat and sleek-looking; they painted their bodies all over; they had great holes bored in their ears; and wore, as did the others, aprons made of bark, or palm-leaves. They had a habit of anointing themselves from head to foot, with oil of cocoa-nuts and sesame, in order, as they said, to pro-tect them from the sun and wind. Some of the chief men were arrayed in long gowns made of cotton, the ends of which were fringed with a kind of silk; their weapons were daggers and knives, the hilts, in some cases, ornamented with gold; and for fishing, they had harpoons and nets.

These savages had one habit which greatly disgusted Magellan and his companions. This was their habit of betel-chewing. A sort of pear-shaped fruit, called areca, grew on the islands. This, with some lime, they would wrap up in the betel-leaves, and putting it into their mouths, would chew eagerly by the hour together. It had the effect of keeping them continually excited ; but when the Spaniards tasted it, it made them very sick.

Magellan remained among the Philippines a week. The ships fortunately needed but few repairs; and the great fruitfulness of the islands supplied him with an ample abundance of provisions. The two springs on the little island yielded plenty of good water ; and the forests on the larger islands afforded an excellent stock of wood. It seemed as if the trials of the wanderers were passed, and as if the rest of their voyage were to be a holiday sail.

CHAPTER X.

MAGELLAN AMONG THE MALAYS.

T was now the latter part of March; in that tropical region one of the pleasant-est periods of the year, when the sun no longer blazed down remorselessly, and the superb vegetation of the equatorial lands displayed its gaudiest colors.

As the ships wound in among clusters of islands, which were now never out of sight a single day, Magellan thought he had never seen so many natural beauties, that he had never imagined such trees, and shrubs, and flowers, so glowing an atmosphere, so smooth and fair a sea ; such beauti-ful forests, jungles, valleys, such fairy isles, as he now beheld.

He often sat on deck at sunrise, and gazed on the magic scene ; observed the lovely islands as one after another was passed ; saw the natives as they ran about on the shore, or huddled in curious groups to watch the ships; and inhaled the rich, dense perfumes that the breezes wafted from the fruitful fields.

After skirting many islands, the fleet came, one night, near an island where a great fire appeared to be burning. The next morning Magellan anchored just off its shores; and no sooner had he done so, than a boat with eight men pulled out from the island, and approached the "Trinidad." When it came near, a Malay, whom Magellan had brought with him as an interpreter, exclaimed in an excited voice, that the men in the boat were his countrymen, and that he would speak to them. Magellan told him to do so; and the Malay, leaning over the side of the ship, rattled off some gibberish at the top of his lungs. The men in the boat, as soon as they heard him, jumped up and began to make wild gesticulations; and when he paused, replied to him in the same tongue. The interpreter asked them to come on board the "Trinidad;" but they replied that they were afraid to do so.

Then Magellan caused a small plank to be brought; to this he tied a red cap, and some trinkets, and threw it into the water near the boat. The natives seized the plank eagerly; and the chief of them, detaching the cap, put it on his shaggy head, and began dancing about in the boat.

Presently they rowed rapidly away; and Magellan was about to weigh anchor and proceed on his voyage, when he saw two larger boats, with many more men in them, put out from the shore. As the foremost drew near the "Trinidad," he perceived in the centre of it a tall, dark man, much more richly dressed than his companions, seated under an awning of mats. He asked the interpreter who this man could be; the Malay replied that he was doubtless the king of the island. Such, indeed, he proved; for the Malay addressed him in his own language, to which the swarthy monarch readily replied. He could not be prevailed upon to trust his royal person on board the flag-ship; but sent some of his courtiers, whom Magellan cordially welcomed, and to whom he confided some presents for the king. In return, the king sent him a large bar of solid gold, which made the eyes of the sailors sparkle; and a basket of ginger.

Finding this native prince so friendly, Magellan resolved to prolong his stay at the island, which was called Mazzava. The ships moved around into a convenient cove, quite near the royal residence; and now, every day, civilities passed between the natives and the Spaniards. The king was soon persuaded to go on board the "Trinidad;" and on his arrival, in great state, one morning, he went up to Magellan, and tenderly embraced him. The Admiral had an arm-chair placed on deck for his august visitor, and entered into familiar conversation with him, the Malay acting as interpreter. The king said that he wished to be "cassi, cassi," with Magellan—that is, the best of friends; and in token of his amiable disposition, he produced some china dishes, on which were rice and fish.

Magellan was not to be outdone in generosity and politeness; he gave the king a robe of red and yellow cloth, and a handsomely embroidered red cap; seeing to it that presents of knives and mirrors were also made to the king's attendants. Magellan then caused cloths of different colors, linen, and coral to be brought and shown to his guest; and ordered the artillery to be fired, which much pleased the king, who, having heard guns fired before, was not terrified. The king, seeing one of the Spaniards with a suit of armor on, asked what was the purpose of so strange an attire; whereupon Magellan ordered three other Spaniards to strike the man in armor with swords and daggers, as hard as they could. The king observing that they made no impression on him, then understood why armor was worn.

Magellan took care to let the swarthy monarch know that he had two hundred men who, thus clad in armor, could fight without being harmed by any enemy's weapons.

Resolved to show the king still further evidence of the powers of the Europeans in battle, he commanded two of his soldiers to engage in a mock combat in fencing. The potentate leaned forward in his chair, and gazed breathlessly at the struggle. He seemed amazed at the skill with which the soldiers parried each other's blows, and aimed rapid and deadly thrusts at each other's breasts. He examined the swords, cuirasses and hemlets which were brought for his inspection, with the deepest interest.

Then, turning to Magellan, whom he was be-

ginning to regard as something more than mortal, he asked if he had made a long voyage, and
how he was able to navigate his great ships
hither? Magellan then showed the king his charts,
compass, quadrants, and other instruments, and
explained their use as well as he could; and
made the king stare with wonder, when he told
him that he had sailed for many months without seeing a speck of land in any direction.

The royal visit was brought to a close by a
bountiful repast in the Admiral's cabin, at which
the best things the ships afforded, or that had
been procured on the islands, were served, daintily
prepared and cooked by the stewards of the fleet.
The king tasted of all the dishes, eating some of
them with a keen relish, and making wry faces at
others. He disdained the use of knives and
forks, but ate fast with his fingers. He became
very merry after drinking some port wine, to
which he took a vast liking, and once more embracing Magellan, swore eternal friendship for
him and his mighty sovereignty, the king of
Spain.

A day or two after, it was arranged that two
of Magellan's principal men should go on shore,

visit the king's house, and see the town and the the natives. One of these was Antonio Pigafetta, an accomplished, courtly Italian, a cherished friend of Magellan; who, years afterwards, wrote the best account that exists of Magellan's voyage and exploits.

As soon as Pigafetta and his companion had landed on the island, the king approached them, and lifted his hands to the sky; and they did the same. This, it appears, was the way the king had of saying, "You are right welcome." Then he conducted his visitors to an inlet, the shores of which grew thick with tall canes, and where a long boat was moored; and made motions to them to step on board, and take their seats on the little deck in the aft end. The royal at-tendants stood around, with their swords and spears. Presently some roast pig and wine were brought, and with these his majesty regaled them. Pigafetta noticed that whenever there was any wine left in the cups, it was poured back carefully into the vase again. The islanders were evidently very economical. Their way of drink-ing was curious. They first raised their hands aloft; then took the cup in their right hand, while

they held out the left towards their companions. The king, just before drinking, clinched
his fist, and thrust it close to Pigafetta's face;
but the latter, perceiving that it was a friendly,
and not a hostile motion, returned the singular
compliment.

When the two guests had feasted to the top
of their bent off roast pig, rice, and broth, they
were conducted to the royal palace. A poor-look-
ing palace, indeed, it was; a long, ricketty building, which reminded Pigafetta of the barns in his
own country, thatched with fig and palm-leaves.
It rested on heavy timbers and posts, and a flight
of steps reached to its first story from the outside. On entering the chief apartment of the
king, Pigafetta observed a plain floor, covered
with mats, and supplied with rude, low tables.

No sooner were the strangers, the king, and
the courtiers seated on the mats, than more food
and drink was brought. These people seemed,
indeed, forever eating and drinking. This time
Pigafetta and his comrade were treated to roast
fish and ginger, which really tasted quite nice.
Pigafetta's companion, indeed, enjoyed his supper
so much, especially the wine—which was far

more palatable than that they had got at the other
islands—that he grew very tipsy; and made so
much noise that Pigafetta was obliged to have
him carried to one corner of the room, and laid
on a mat.   Here he was soon snoring soundly,
in a deep slumber.

Presently the prince, the king's son and heir,
a comely, cream-colored young man, came in, and
his father made him sit at Pigafetta's side.   As
soon as it was dark, torches made of the gum of
a tropical tree, and wrapped in palm and fig-
leaves, were brought and lighted; and these lit
up a very curious and unwonted scene.   The king
now went away to his own sleeping-apartment,
leaving the prince with Pigafetta, to sleep in that
where they had supped.   On retiring his majesty
kissed Pigafetta's hands.

The Italian found his bed to consist of some
pillows and cushions stuffed with leaves.   It was
a rough place for repose; but, having been used
to the trials of the sea, he minded it little, and
slept soundly until he was awakened by some of
the royal attendants.   He and his companion
breakfasted gayly with the king; and while they
were at the table, there appeared another potent-

ate, a brother of their host, who was the king of a neighboring island. This personage impressed Pigafetta very much. He was a tall and very handsome man, with raven-black hair that fell in thick clusters about his shoulders, and a dark, copper complexion, large and brilliant black eyes, and an erect and symmetrical figure. Upon his head he wore a kind of turban of rich silk, finely embroidered; he was attired in a silken tunic that reached his knees; two enormous gold rings hung from his ears; at his side was suspended a dagger, the handle of which was solid gold, and the sheath carved wood; while his person exhaled a strong and agreeable perfume. When this king spoke, Pigafetta perceived that on each of his teeth were stuck little round disks of gold, which made his mouth fairly shine when he opened it. Pigafetta was told that the island on which he ruled had gold mines, from which great nuggets of the precious metal were often extracted.

Pigafetta and his companion then returned to the flag-ship, carrying this monarch with them. Magellan received him as cordially as he had received his brother, and he went away fully as much delighted with the Spaniards as his brother had been. Easter had now come, and Magellan, who was a good Catholic, and through-out his voyage had never omitted to observe each festivity of the Church as it came, resolved to have a solemn mass performed, in honor of the anniversary of the rising of Christ. He therefore sent a message to the king of Mazzava, inform-ing him that the voyagers were going on shore, not to visit him, but to hold a religious festival. He invited the two kings and their courtiers to be present, and to join in the devotions of the Europeans, if they saw fit.

It was an impressive scene on that brilliant, warm Easter Sunday morning, on the shore of a tropical isle, with its lofty palms and luxuriant shrubs growing almost to the water's edge; thousands of miles from the nearest Christian church, in the midst of regions given over to idol worship and the densest barbarism! There were the weather-beaten sailors, rough and rude, attired in such show of good clothing as they could still afford; there were the officers, in more imposing costume, their swords hung at their sides, their velvet cloaks thrown across their shoulders, their heads adorned with sashed and plumed caps; there was Magellan, with serious countenance, awaiting the beginning of the rite; and there, strangest of all, stood the two swarthy kings, with painted faces, decked out in fantastic and savage finery, surrounded by their dark-featured and half-nude courtiers, watching with keen interest the scene that was being enacted before them. On the smooth strand an altar had been set up, with lighted candles, and lace draperies, and such other ornaments as had been brought for religious purposes on the voyage; and before it now appeared two priests, with shaven heads and long embroidered copes.

Just before the mass began, Magellan advanced to the two kings; and taking his place between them, gently sprinkled them with musk-rose water. Then the cannon boomed from the ships; and this deafening noise was succeeded by the clear voices of the priests rising in the intonation of the sacred words. At one period of the ceremony, the Christians went forward and kissed a cross, held by one of the priests; and their example was followed by the barbarian monarchs and their subjects. When the host was elevated,

all, including the natives, prostrated themselves
on the ground; and at this moment the cannon
once more pealed forth from the decks of the
ships.

Mass over, Magellan ordered that the more
lively and worldly festivities should begin; and
the kings watched with wonder and delight the
skilful fencing, and the rough martial sports, in
which the Spaniards now lustily engaged. They
were amazed at the strength of the wrestlers;
witnessed breathlessly the shooting matches, for
which targets were set up on the strand; and
looked on eagerly while rough games of many
kinds were played by the strangers.

There was one more task for Magellan to per-
form, ere he left these hospitable isles. He was
now in regions, the discovery and possession of
which Spain and Portugal disputed between
them. Although himself by birth a Portuguese,
Magellan owed now his allegiance to the king
·of Spain, who had trusted him, and confided
to him the command of the fleet. As the two
countries aspired to divide the eastern world between them, it was necessary for him to have a
care for the interests of the sovereign he served,

and to take possesion of the places where he landed.

Not **very** far from the shore where mass had been celebrated, rose a lofty and verdant hill, the summit of which, however, was quite bare. It was the highest eminence on the island; the top could be discerned from a great distance, by a ship at sea. Upon the summit Magellan resolved to erect a cross, surmounted by a wooden crown, as a token that he had taken possession of the island in the name of the Spanish king.

It was not difficult to persuade the king of Mazzava to allow him to do this. The barbarian monarch was told that King Charles had commanded such crosses to be raised wherever his voyagers went; that if, in future, any Spanish ships came to Mazzava, they would know, by the cross, that it was a friendly country, and would commit no violence on the people; and that if any of his subjects were ever ill-treated by Spaniards, they would make full reparation, as soon as the cross was shown to them.

Magellan did not forget to add a pious lesson to these persuasions. He assured his royal host that the cross was the symbol of the Christian deity; and that, if he and his people would, at the approach of danger, fall down and adore it, no harm could come to them; neither thunder, lightning, nor tempest could injure them.

The king and his brother, the other king, readily consented that the cross should be erected; whereupon Magellan, attended by fifty of his sturdiest men, armed to the teeth, several of whom carried the heavy cross, slowly ascended the hill. With him went the two kings and their retinues.

Arrived at the summit, the Spaniards dug a deep hole; the cross was placed in position, and the hole was filled up. Magellan advanced, and knelt before the cross a moment; then, rising, and taking off his cap, he declared the island to be the dominion of the king of Spain.

Soon after, Magellan went to bid adieu to the two monarchs, who overwhelmed him, not only with an affectionate reception, which they ex-pressed by touching his forehead and kissing his hands, but with an abundance of the good things their fruitful land afforded. They described the islands by which he would pass on his way, told him of the traits of their inhabitants, which to avoid, and in which he might expect a hospitable welcome; and at the last moment, the king of Mazzava resolved to accompany him, at least as far as the inland of Sebu.

The ships were now provided, not only with grain, water, and wood, but an ample store of figs, cocoanuts, lemons, pigs, fowl, ginger and rice; what few repairs they needed were completed; and on a pleasant morning in April, Magellan sailed away from Mazzava, delighted with the reception he had met with there, and his heart buoyant with the hope of a successful continuation and ending of his voyage. With him, on board the flag-ship, went the king of Mazzava, and several of his courtiers.

CHAPTER XI.

ADVENTURES AT SEBU.

THE island of Sebu, Magellan was told, was the most beautiful and fruitful of the vast labyrinth of islands which cluster in the Archipelago. It lay some leagues westward of Mazzava; and was ruled over by one of the most intelligent and powerful potentates in the Eastern seas.

To this island, therefore, he determined to repair. It would be one of the fairest provinces which he could offer to King Charles; and he would do all in his power to engage the friendship and alliance of its ruler.

On the way, the weather was pleasant, and no accident occurred to mar the pleasure of the voyage. Magellan conversed much, through the Malay interpreter, with the friendly king who had trusted himself with him, and learned many curious things about the peoples and customs of the islands by which they sailed.

The adventurers observed everything with the deepest interest; and many were the strange sights and scenes which, in this far-off region, greeted their eyes. They saw birds flying through the air, "as large as eagles," one of which they killed, and ate with good relish ; they saw doves of various brilliant hues, parrots with gorgeous plumage, and long-tailed blackbirds as large as hens; while on the shores of the islands they espied tortoises which, compared with those of Europe, were enormous.

It was on a Sunday, about noon, that the fleet came in sight of the much talked-of island of Sebu. Skirting its shores, the Spaniards saw many closely-built and busy villages, some close to the beach, others nestled in picturesque valleys, at the foot of green, sloping hills. They sailed for some distance along the coast, until finally they reached a pretty bay, at the head of which was situated the principal town of the island.

As the ships entered the bay, Magellan ordered that the standards should be run up to the masthead, the sails lowered, and the cannon fired. A vast crowd of natives speedily assembled along the shore. When they heard the deafening report of the cannon, echoing among the hills, they huddled together in a terrified mass, and made all haste to regain the town.

Magellan then sent an intelligent young Portuguese whom he had brought with him, and the Malay interpreter, on shore, to seek the presence of the king of Sebu, and assure him that the fleet had come on a friendly errand.

As they advanced from the shore, and approached the town, they saw the inhabitants fleeing from them in all directions, and shutting themselves up in their houses. The young Portuguese, however, succeeded in overtaking one old man, who could not move as fast as the rest; and made him know, through the interpreter, what his errand was. The old man soon recovered from his fright, and said he would go and deliver the message of the strangers to his sovereign. In no long time he returned, and told the Portuguese and his companion to follow him into the royal presence.

They found the king seated on a wide mat, in

a court of his palace ; which was a low building,
erected in the form of a quadrangle. He was
surrounded by a multitude of courtiers ; while at
his feet lay, in languid attitudes, his dark-brown
wives, whose raven hair fell on their shoulders,
and whose large black eyes stared curiously at
the white men.

The Malay interpreter advanced and knelt before the king, who lifted his hands heavenward
in token of welcome. Then the Malay spoke in
his own tongue, which the king understood at
once. He was assured that the fleet had come
on an errand of peace and good-will.

"What, then," asked the monarch, "are you
seeking here?"

"My master," replied the Malay, "is a captain
of the greatest king in the world, and hath come,
by his king's command, to discover the far-famed
Molucca islands. Hearing of your courtesy and
good renown, he has come hither to visit you,
and to exchange the merchandize he has brought
for such provisions as you are willing to provide
him."

"Your master," responded the shrewd prince,
"is right welcome. But we have a custom, that

all ships that enter our port pay tribute. Only four days ago, a ship came here from Siam, laden with gold and slaves, and paid the tribute I exacted. Here," added the king, "is a Siamese merchant who came in her." So saying, he pointed to a strange-looking personage, with sallow face and squinting eyes, but very richly dressed, who was standing by.

"But my captain," replied the Malay, drawing himself up proudly, "will not pay tribute to any sovereign in the world; being, as he is, the subject of the greatest of them. If you wish peace, you shall have it. But if you had rather have war, it shall be so."

The brow of the dusky potentate darkened at this bold reply, and for a moment he seemed on the point of ordering the strangers to be seized. He looked around among his people, and half-rose from his mat. His hand was already clutching a short sword which hung at his girdle, and the Portuguese and Malay had grasped their daggers, when the Siamese merchant, coming forward, and making a profound salaam, spoke:

"Look well, O king," said he, "to what you do. These people are the same that conquered

Calicut, Malacca, and all the greater India. If you receive them hospitably, and proffer them of your abundant good things, you will find yourself the better for it. They will be your friends and allies. But if you treat them ill, it will be all the worse for you ; so the people of Calicut have found out, to their cost."

"My sovereign," added the interpreter, who had understood all that the Siamese had said, "is a much greater ruler than the king of Portugal, who conquered India. He is not only king of Spain, but emperor of Christendom. If you do not well treat his captain, he will, another time, send hither enough men and ships to sweep you and your subjects off the face of the earth."

These speeches seemed to impress the king of Sebu very much ; he declared that he would talk with his chief advisers, and would deliver his response to Magellan's messengers the next day. He then gave proof that he had recovered his good temper, by ordering a bountiful feast to be set before the white men ; who soon after returned to the flag-ship, and apprized Magellan of what had passed.

The next day the messengers returned to the

island, where the king received them in a large,
open space, between the houses. He was squatted on a palm mat, and was quite naked, except
that he had a wide cloth about his waist, and a
loose turban, embroidered with silk, on his head.
About his neck hung a heavy chain, while in his
ears were two gold rings, studded with precious
stones. The king was a little, fat, jovial-looking
man, though the expression of his countenance
was marred by tatooing. When the visitors approached, he was eating tortoise eggs from some
china dishes; taking, every now and then, a long
drink from a jug of palm wine, which he sucked
through a cane tube. Asking them to sit by
him, he proceeded at once to overwhelm them
with questions, which he asked eagerly, bending
towards the interpreter to catch his replies.

Was there more than one commander in the
ships? Was he to be required to pay tribute?
How many men were there on board? and so on.
The young Portuguese replied that Magellan did
not ask any tribute, but only desired to trade
with the articles he had brought from Spain.
The king seemed at last fully satisfied ; for, prick-
ing his right arm, he let a little blood flow upon

a fig-leaf, and wrapping it up, begged the Portuguese to carry it to Magellan, as a token that he would be a faithful friend of the king of Spain. He asked a similar token from the Admiral which the Portuguese smilingly promised.

After this, everything went on swimmingly between the voyagers and the people of Sebu. The king of Mazzava went ashore on a visit to his brother monarch, and on his return, told Magellan that the king of Sebu was preparing a large quantity of provisions for him; and that in the afternoon two young princes, nephews of the king, with their retinues, would come on board to present them.

Magellan prepared to welcome these young princes in a manner worthy of their rank and importance, and to show his gratitude for the good things they brought. A handsome carpet was spread on the deck, and mats were laid on either side. On the carpet was placed a red velvet chair for Magellan himself; and leather chairs, for the other captains and officers, were ranged on the mats. The standards floated from the masts; and the flag-ship presented a gay, holiday aspect.

About the middle of the afternoon the boats

conveying the princes were seen to put out from the shore; Magellan and the rest took their places; and soon the dusky and gaudily-dressed group were seated in front of the Admiral. At Magellan's side stood the faithful Malay interpreter, who rendered his conversation with the princes easy.

"Is it your custom," asked Magellan, of the elder and more important of the princes, "to speak in public about matters of state? And have you the power to conclude peace between us and the king of Sebu?"

The prince bowed assent to both these questions.

"Then I would have you know," resumed Magellan, "that I ardently desire this peace, and will pray God to confirm it."

"I hear the captain's words with delight," was the prince's answer; "I have never heard a stranger speak so gently."

Magellan then questioned his royal guest about many things. He asked, "Who will succeed your king, on his death?"

"The king has no son," was the reply, "but several daughters. I am the king's nephew, and have married his eldest daughter; and I shall be his successor."

The prince also told him that when fathers and mothers in Sebu grew old, they were greatly neglected, and their children ordered them about as if they were slaves.

The discoverers and conquerors of the days in which Magellan lived thought it one of their first duties to convert the heathen peoples whom they encountered to Christianity. They sometimes did this by persuasion; and not seldom by force. When the savage kings and their peoples refused to abandon their religion for that of the European, they were often compelled to accept the new faith by fire and sword.

Magellan, therefore, lost no opportunity of trying to plant Christianity among the rude natives of the tropical isles; and the first task to accomplish was to convert their rulers.

He now began to persuade the young princes to embrace the Christian religion. Reproving them for the ill-treatment which they declared the old people suffered in their kingdom, he said:

"Our God, who made heaven and earth, and all things therein, has commanded that every

oi.e should yield obedience and respect to his
father and mother; and you may be sure that
whoever does otherwise shall be condemned to
eternal fire."

The princes listened earnestly to all that he
said, and finally declared that, if the king would
consent, they would become Christians.

"You must not accept our faith," said Magellan, "from fear of us, or in order to please us.
If you wish to become Christians, you must do
so willingly. No harm shall be done you if you
do not embrace our religion; but those who do,
shall be more loved, and better treated, than the
others. Moreover, if you become Christians, I
will leave you arms, as my king has commanded,
with which to defend yourselves from your
enemies."

The princes declared that they would embrace
Christianity of their own free wills; whereupon
Magellan, with tears in his eyes, warmly embraced them, and caused the priests to bless
them. All on board now sat down to a bountiful feast; after which the princes and Magellan
exchanged presents. The princes brought forth
a large basket of rice, figs, goats, and fowl; and

Magellan returned to them cloth, red caps, and cups of gilt glass, besides a robe of yellow and violet silk for their royal uncle.

The young Portuguese and the Malay were now sent on shore every day to converse with the king, to arrange for a treaty of peace, to establish trade, and to prepare the monarch and his courtiers for their reception into the Christian faith. They were treated, whenever they went, with trust and hospitality. On one occasion, the elder of the young princes conducted them to his house, where he provided various amusements for them. Among these was a very pretty dance, performed by four lovely young girls; who, as they danced, played softly and sweetly upon musical instruments, the like of which the Portuguese had never before seen. Another time, when one of the Spanish sailors had died, he was carried on shore by the two messengers to be buried. The king not only provided him with a grave in the open space in the centre of the town, but himself, with his court, attended the funeral ceremony. After the sailor was buried, his comrades set up a cross over the grave.

The Spaniards were soon engaged in an active trade with the people of Sebu. The king provided one of the larger huts, near the shore, as a warehouse; and thither was carried a variety of the goods that composed the cargo of the ships. Four of the Spaniards were selected to act as salesmen. They bartered iron, cloths, and trinkets for gold, which, it appeared, was found in large quantities in Sebu and the neighboring islands; and in dealing with the natives they found them peaceable, honest, and fair, and not at all disposed to drive a hard bargain. They had a curious contrivance for weighing their goods. It consisted of a wooden pole suspended in the middle, with a basin suspended by three cords at one end, and a cord at the other, upon which hung a weight equal to the basin, to which the weights were attached. The Spaniards soon persuaded the natives to give up this cumbrous device for the scales they had brought with them from Europe. The natives gave gold worth fifteen Spanish ducats, for fourteen pounds of iron.

CHAPTER XII.

THE BARBARIANS CONVERTED.

THE king and his court were, in no long time, fully persuaded to become Christians; and Magellan resolved to make the ceremony of their baptism and entrance into the fold of the Church as imposing and impressive as possible. He wished that their untutored minds should have the deepest sense of the importance of the step they were taking, so that they would never forget or retreat from it.

Preparations for the solemn event were made on the most elaborate scale. A high platform was erected by the Spaniards in the centre of the open space; and this was decked out with tapestry, carpets, and palm branches. Not only the king of Sebu, but his queen, and the king of Mazzava (who was still with Magellan) were to be baptized; and the day appointed was Sunday, the fourteenth of April.

On that morning, all was commotion, both in the fleet and in the town. The natives assembled in the streets, and huddled in excited groups along the beach; while the crews of the ships attired themselves in their best suits, as if for an extraordinary occasion.

Soon everything was ready. The boats were lowered, and each was filled with its quota of officers and sailors; and when all had embarked, the boats set out for the shore. At the same time the cannon broke the stillness of the Sunday morning, and sent joyous peals over the waters. The boats that went ahead contained forty men in armor, one of whom carried the royal standard of Spain. These landed first, and were soon followed by the sailors. A procession was formed; Magellan was in front, with his captains, all wearing velvet cloaks and plumed caps; then came the priests; the soldiers were next in order; and the rear was occupied by the crews.

Advancing up the slight slope that led from the shore to the open space, Magellan and his company reached the scene of the day's ceremony.

The short, fat king, in fantastic attire, his face freshly painted that morning, stood ready to receive them, surrounded by a numerous array of courtiers and chiefs. By his side was the king of Mazzava, who had preceded the Spaniards on shore.

Magellan and the two barbarian kings now ascended the scaffold, and took their places in chairs of red and violet velvet, which had been brought from the flag-ship for the purpose. Meanwhile, the chief men of Sebu arranged themselves on chairs, or squatted on mats, below the platform; the trumpets sent forth a loud, long blast; then Magellan, turning to the potentates, and addressing them through the Malay, who stood behind his chair, for the last time asked them if they really wished to become good Christians.

"If you do," said he, "you must burn all the idols in your dominions; and in their places, set up the cross, which is the symbol of our God. And each day you and your people must go and kneel at the cross, and join your hands, and implore the favor of heaven. Will you do this?"

The kings promptly replied that they would; and that whatever the "captain," as they called

The Baptism of the King. — Page 175.

Magellan, commanded, they would faithfully and always obey.

Magellan then rose, and taking the king of Sebu by the hand, led him around the platform; after which the priests performed the solemn ceremony of baptism. The king was christened by the name of Charles, after the king of Spain. The king of Mazzava, and the eldest of the Sebu princes, were next in the like manner baptized; the former receiving the name of John, and the latter that of Ferdinand.

The principal subjects of the king of Sebu now flocked upon the platform, to be received in their turn into the bosom of the Catholic Church; and when fifty of them had been baptized, the rite of the mass was performed. Then Magellan and his company returned to the ships, being escorted to the beach by their royal host.

In the afternoon a ceremony not less curious and impressive was performed. This was the baptism of the queen of Sebu, and the dusky ladies of her court. One of the priests, accompanied by Pigafetta and some others, went on shore, and were met in the open space by the queen and her companions. These were led upon the platform, where the queen was conducted to a cushioned seat. She was young and pretty, and was arrayed in a black and white robe; her mouth and nails were very red, and she wore on her head a large hat made of palm-leaves, surmounted with a sort of crown, also made of palm-leaves.

The priest, in the midst of a large multitude of Sebu men and women, who looked on with excited interest, approached the queen, and held up before her a small wooden image of the Virgin and Child, and also a cross. The queen seemed impressed with these, and through the interpreter declared her willingness to become a Christian and to be baptized. The priests therefore sprinkled water on her raven locks, and called her by the name of Joan, after the Spanish king's mother. Her daughter, a young girl of fourteen, who advanced very timidly up the steps, was next in like manner received into the Church, being called Catherine; and the queen of Mazzava was baptized as Isabella.

As the queen was withdrawing she begged the priest to give her "the little wooden boy," meaning the image of Christ, to put in place of her idols, which she promised to destroy. This the priest did willingly. Many years after, on the return of the Spaniards to Sebu with missionaries, they found the little image still in the town, and the natives worshipping it as an idol; whereupon the missionaries taught them its true significance, blessed it, and had it placed in the Christian church that was built. From having found this image there, these Spanish missionaries named the place, " the City of Jesus," by which it is still known.

Before the shades of night had fallen, no less than eight hundred natives, including the royal family and the court, had been baptized, and the country had become, in name at least, a Christian one ; and Magellan thought well to celebrate so remarkable a conversion by festivities in the evening. By the brilliant light of the moon, the king, queen, and court of Sebu came down to the beach, whither Magellan had caused one of his cannon to be brought; it was fired off on the waves; and now that the barbarians knew what it meant, and that they need not be frightened, they listened with delight, with much shouting,

capering, and dancing about, to the sudden shocks
and echoing reverberations.

Magellan did not confine the baptisms to the
first day ; but every day after that, for more than
a week, the ceremony was performed over crowds
of natives who flocked to receive it. It was a
strange sight to see the groups of dark islanders,
with their painted faces and palm-leaf aprons,
kneeling at the feet of the priests, and with
amazed and wondering eyes watching his every action ; and, their turn over, scampering down
the steps, and dancing wildly about on the sward,
and under the wide-spreading trees. It is not
probable that any of them got a clear conception
of what it was to be a Christian. They only
knew that their king had accepted the new religion ; they felt awe towards the Spaniards,
whom they looked upon as more than mortal ;
their barbaric fondness for show and ceremony
was gratified by the stately rite which they saw
the priests going through ; and they cared little,
apparently, for their own rude wooden gods and
goddesses.

A cross was now set up in the centre of the
town ; and every day mass was said near it, which

Magellan usually himself attended, explaining, through the Malay interpreter, such points in the Christian religion as he thought he could make his benighted hearers understand.

One day, the queen of Sebu came to hear mass in all her state. She was attired in black and white, and wore a long silk veil with gold stripes, flowing down gracefully over her shoulders. Before her went three young girls, each carrying one of the queen's palm-leaf hats. Following the queen, flocked a great number of women of rank, wearing smaller veils, and hats above them. Otherwise, they only wore a palm-leaf apron about their waists; while their long black hair fell in luxuriant clusters over their shoulders to their knees.

The queen approached the altar, and knelt before it, and then took her place on a large silk-embroidered ottoman; while her chief ladies surrounded her in a semi-circle. Magellan advancing to her, gently sprinkled over her and her companions some rose-water and musk, which they sniffed eagerly, as if much pleased by the perfume; and then mass was said by the priests.

On another occasion, Magellan resolved that,

at the mass, the king of Sebu should, with all due formality, swear allegiance to the king of Spain. This ceremony, he thought, should be made as impressive as possible. The king made his appearance at the appointed hour, in a long silk robe, with which Magellan had provided him ; and with him came his two brothers, and many of his principal courtiers. These being ranged in a row on seats before the altar, Magellan, standing before an image of the Virgin, drew his sword, and holding it aloft, called upon the king to take the oath to be ever faithful and true to the Spanish sovereign. The king bowed his head, and repeated, in his own tongue, the words of the oath that Magellan offered him. Magellan then affectionately embraced him, at the same time saying that when a man took such an oath as that, he should rather die than fail to keep it. In his turn, he swore to be always faithful, to be true to the king of Sebu, in the name of the Virgin and of King Charles. Then, turning to his men, Magellan ordered them to bring forth a splendid velvet chair ; this he presented to the swarthy monarch.

"Wherever you go," said Magellan, "have

this throne borne before you, by your attendants, as a sign of your power and sovereignty."

In return, and as a token that he would keep
his oath, the king presented Magellan with some
large gold rings, for the ears, fingers, and ankles,
all of which were set with roughly-cut precious
stones.

A day or two after, Magellan was visiting the
town, and going about in company with the
king, when, on reaching one of the rude native
temples, he saw, to his disgust, that the idols
were still in their places, and that the people
were worshipping them. Turning sharply to his
royal companion, he asked him what this meant?

"You have promised," he said, "to destroy
these idols. Why have you not done so?'

The king replied that he intended to burn the
idols; but that one of his nephews, a valiant
warrior, lay very ill, and that they were praying
to the idols to restore him to health.

"If you wish to see him well again," rejoined
Magellan, "you will at once burn all these fool-
ish idols, which can do nothing for him; and you
will cause your sick nephew to be baptized. I
will wager my head that he will then speedily

recover." So great was Magellan's faith in miracles!

"It shall be done," was the king's reply.

Thereupon, a solemn procession was formed, which repaired to the sick prince's house. The prince was, indeed, very low. He could neither speak nor move; his eyes stared unmeaningly at the priests, nor did he seem to recognize any one or anything. He was carefully lifted from the soft mat on which he lay, into a sitting posture; and was thus baptized. Two of his wives and his ten children also submitted to the rite.

Not very long after, Magellan approached the sick man, and addressed him in a few words of his own language. The prince slowly moved his head, and muttered something. Magellan applied some brandy to his lips. In a few moments the invalid grew so much better that he could move freely, and talk quite rationally ; and from that time he grew gradually better.

This incident was hailed by all the Spaniards as a great miracle; and they took care to impress its meaning, as they interpreted it, upon the minds of the natives.

It happened that some of the native old women,

who had refused to be converted, had concealed an idol in the sick prince's house, thinking that this would restore him to health. On his recovery, the prince discovered the idol, hid behind some mats in a corner. He forthwith brought it out, and had it burned in presence of the king and all his subjects. Not content with this—for he himself was fully persuaded that the Christians had performed a miracle on him—he set fire to the temples that stood on the sea-shore; while the people gathered in crowds to see the conflagration, shouted loudly, and aided him in his work of destruction. The idols thus burned were made of wood, and were curved in shape, being hollowed out behind; they had large faces, painted, with four large teeth, like those of a wild boar; their legs and arms were stretched out horizontally, and their feet turned upwards, like the feet of the Chinese. They were, indeed, hideous-looking objects.

While Magellan was at Sebu, a very curious ceremony was performed by the natives. This was what was called " the sacrifice of the swine," or " blessing the pig." Their mode of blessing the pig was an odd one, as will be seen; and Magel-

lan and his companions witnessed the performance with much interest.

The whole population gathered in or about the
large open space in the centre of the town, which
evidently served as the spot where all public
ceremonies took place. The king and queen sat
on cushions raised on a platform; and Magellan
and his captains were stationed on either side of
the royal couple. Presently a loud, banging
noise was heard, and a number of the natives
appeared, violently thumping upon tambours, or
drums. They were followed by others, who bore
large dishes, two of which were filled with cakes
of rice and cooked millet, and roast fish, and the
third with cloths and strips of palm bark.

One of the cloths was spread on the ground,
before the king; and two old women now made
their entrance, fantastically dressed, and vigorously blowing upon rude reed trumpets. These
old women, stepping upon the carpet, and turning to the sun, made that luminary a profound
obeisance; then taking the other cloths that had
been brought, they arrayed themselves in them.
One twisted a cloth about her head, so that the
knots formed two horns, on either side; having

done which she began to dance and sing, and stretch out her arms towards the sun.

The other, attiring herself in the palm cloths, followed her companion's example, with shrill shrieking and wild gestures; each tooting, every now and then, on her reed trumpet. While this was going on, a fat pink pig was brought into the open space, and bound securely to a stake; upon which the old women began to caper around the poor animal, which squealed, in his terror, with all his might.

The next thing the old women did was to make a short prayer, in low, mumbling voices, to the sun. Then one of them—the first who had appeared—took from an attendant a cup of wine, which she handed to her companion. The latter took it and raised it three or four times to her lips, as if to drink it; but always withdrew it, and resumed her droning prayer. At last, all of a sudden, she dashed the wine on the poor pig, which squealed more frantically than ever.

Throwing away the empty cup, the old woman now seized a long limber lance, with a point made of a sharpened fish-bone, and leaped from end to end of the carpet, brandishing the lance and gnashing her teeth as she went. Approaching the pig, she made thrusts with the lance, as if to plunge it into him; but withdrew it again, and resumed her strange dance. Pretty soon, however, she carried her threat into execution; for, poising the lance a moment in her hand, and with rapid glance taking perfect aim, she shot it straight through the quivering creature's heart. Withdrawing it at once, she retired; whereupon two male natives seized the pig, closed the wound, and dressed it with herbs. The old woman who had done the deed now took a lighted torch, and capered about, holding it in her mouth; while her companion, dipping her lance in the pig's blood, carried it to her husband, whose forehead she marked with it, doing the same afterwards to her other relatives. Both old women then took off their robes, and, retreating into a corner, greedily ate the rice-cakes and roast fish by themselves. The pig was afterwards roasted and eaten by the royal party; and Magellan was told that pigs were only eaten in Sebu when they had been killed in this way.

During all the time that the ships were at Sebu, the officers and sailors were wont to go on shore freely, whenever they pleased; and they thus got on very social terms with the natives. They observed that their dusky friends only half-cooked their food, and that they spread a great deal of salt on it. This made them thirsty, and they were constantly drinking the palm wine, which was their favorite beverage. Their method of drinking was to suck the wine from the jars with long reeds. When they saw a knot of sailors they would run to them, and invariably beg them to come and have something to eat and drink.

Once, when a great chief among them died, the Spaniards had an opportunity to witness a Sebu funeral. The chief's corpse was laid in a chest in his house; around the chest was wound a cord, to which branches and leaves were tied in a fantastic fashion; while on the end of each branch, a strip of cotton was fastened. The principal women of the island went to the house of mourning and sat around the corpse, wrapped in white cotton shrouds from head to foot; beside each woman stood a young girl, who wafted a palm-leaf fan before her face. Meanwhile, one of the women was engaged in cutting the hair from the dead man's head with a knife. His favorite wife all this time lay stretched upon his body, with her mouth, hands, and feet pressed close to his. As the woman concluded her hair-cutting, she broke into a low, dismal, wailing song, which the others after awhile caught up. The attendants on the mourners then took procelain vases with burning embers on them, upon which they kept sprinkling myrrh, benzoin, and other perfumes, that formed a cloud of incense in the room.

These ceremonies and mournings continued for several days; meanwhile, the body was anointed with oil of camphor, to preserve it; and at the end of the mourning period, it was solemnly deposited in a kind of tomb, made of wooden logs, in the neighboring forest.

Magellan was delighted with the success which attended his stay at Sebu, which he had prolonged far more than he had intended. It was now time to bid adieu to the friendly king, and proceed on his voyage. As active preparations for setting out were being made, however, an incident occurred which induced Magellan to change his plans, and which was destined to bring a fatal misfortune on the fleet.

The king of Sebu ruled over several islands in the neighborhood of that on which he resided. One of these was Matan, only two or three leagues away. It was a beautiful island, and contained a large and warlike population; and among the chiefs who, under the king, held authority there, was one named Cilapulapu. Just as Magellan was about to sail, another chief in Matan named Zula, came in all haste to Sebu with a message that Cilapulapu, enraged at the conversion of the king and his subjects to Christianity, had rebelled, and had incited the people to rise in revolt. At Matan, he said, all were actively preparing for war against their sovereign. Magellan, on hearing this, resolved that the least he could do would be to remain, and defend the converted king from the violence of his new enemies.

CHAPTER XIII.

A HERO'S DEATH.

MAGELLAN, anxious to confirm the friendly relations which now existed between himself and the king of Sebu, made up his mind that he and his valiant soldiers should alone bear the brunt of the coming conflict; that the sole peril and glory should be theirs of subduing the rebel Cilapulapu. He therefore told the king that he himself would command the attack upon Matan; and that while the king might, if he chose, follow him in his boats, he must refrain from taking part in the fray.

Three of the ships' largest boats were got ready in all haste. On the prow of each was placed a cannon, and sixty of Magellan's bravest and most skilful warriors were detailed to go upon the expedition. These were all armed with corslets and helmets, and carried guns and swords. Magellan ordered that during his absence the fleet should remain under the command of Captain Serrano.

It was just at midnight that the three boats set out for Matan. The night was calm, the sea was still, and the heavens were starlit. Magellan himself went in the foremost boat, and issued his commands in a quick, low voice, as the men rowed swiftly along. His object in starting at midnight was to surprise the enemy, if possible, and effect a landing on the coast of the island before the people there saw him. In the rear of the three boats went a number of the native canoes, of one of which the king himself was an occupant.

Three hours before daylight, the Spaniards arrived off the shores of Matan; it was light enough, however, for Magellan to perceive that the alarm of his coming had already been given. Near the shore, on a hillock, was posted a formidable array of barbarians. Magellan could just discern their long wooden shields, and the moving mass of the savage soldiers. Some traitor had, doubtless, escaped from Sebu in time to apprize Cilapulapu

of his intended attack; and that cunning chief
had lost no time in preparing to receive him.   It
was a strange and alarming sight, to see the
dense ranks of the dusky figures, who, it was not
difficult to perceive, were quite prepared to defend the island.   When the boats came near, they
set up a wild shout, and shook their shields and
spears in token of their hostile temper.

Magellan had taken the precaution to bring
with him a very intelligent Moor, who knew
the Malay tongue (which was spoken in all these
islands), and who had before been at Matan.
This Moor he resolved to send ashore to the
warlike host, with a message of peace and par-
don if they would even now lay down their arms,
and submit to the authority of their lawful monarch.   As the water for some distance from
the shore was very shallow and rocky, the boats
could not approach nearer than the spot where
they had stopped; and the Moor was obliged to
jump in up to his thighs, and wade to the dry land.
As he drew away from the boats, his movements
were watched with breathless interest.   Would
the barbarians attack him, when they saw him
coming alone?   Would they recognize him as a

Moor, or would they take him for a Spaniard? If they allowed him to approach and hold parley with them, how would they receive his message? Would the Moor himself turn traitor, and reveal the numbers and arms of Magellan's men, or would he hold his own counsel, and prove himself a faithful envoy?

These questions rapidly crossed Magellan's mind as, peering through the gloom, he saw the Moor's stalwart form receding and fading as he neared the beachy shore. They were quickly answered by the events which followed. The Moor advanced up the sloping hill; the dusky soldiers made no movement against him. They seemed to be surprised to see him coming, and not at all afraid of him. Presently he seemed to melt into their mass, and was no longer visible.

His stay among them lasted about half an hour, during which the Spaniards watched eagerly for his reappearance. The boats rested quite still on their oars; the silence was profound. At last he emerged from the throng of the islanders, slowly descended the hill again, and waded out to Magellan's boat.

Magellan impatiently awaited his report. The

Moor said that he had been received in a friendly manner, and had been conducted to the chief Cilapulapu. He had then delivered Magellan's message, that, if he would return to his allegiance, all should be forgiven, and the Spaniards would withdraw; otherwise, the rebels would soon feel the sting of their lances. Cilapulapu had replied:

"I will not submit; if the white strangers have lances, so have we, though ours are only lances of reeds. Moreover, we have wooden shields hardened by fire. Let the strangers beware. I only ask that they will not attack us by night. We expect reinforcements, and wish to meet the enemy on even terms. Let them wait till daylight, and then assail us as soon as they please." Magellan perceived, by this insolent message, that gentle means would not be availing. The rebels must be attacked and conquered. He saw, too, that Cilapulapu's request that he should not attack by night, was a cunning device by which he hoped to induce the Spaniards to do that which he asked them not to do. His real desire was that they should make the assault at night; and the reason of this afterwards came to light. Between the shore and their camp and village, the rebels had dug a long, deep ditch. If Magellan had landed and advanced upon them at once, while it was dark, they would have retreated hastily beyond this ditch, and Magellan and his men would have fallen into it.

Magellan therefore patiently waited till daylight. As soon as the first gray of the morning lit up sea and shore, and enabled him to distinguish objects clearly, he gave the order to his little band of troops to get out of the boats and wade rapidly to the beach. By the light of the dawn the enemy could be more distinctly seen; they appeared less formidable than when enveloped by the shroud of night, but they betrayed numbers by no means to be despised. They seemed, moreover, perfectly confident and resolute; and instead of making good their retreat when they saw the Spaniards preparing to go ashore, stood to their position, and were apparently indifferent to the advance of their assailants.

Forty-nine of the Spaniards were designated to make the attack, the remaining eleven being ordered to stay by the boats. Magellan himself was the first to leap into the water. Drawing his sword, he gave the word of command, and in another instant his little force, their swords in their right hands, and their shields borne on their left arms, had gathered around him. Among them was his friend, and afterwards his historian, the Italian Pigafetta. At first their progress through the water was slow, for it was up to their waists. As Magellan boldly went forward, he looked carefully about for a good landing-place; for the beach was interspersed with masses of jagged rock, and it was necessary to avoid the hill on which Cilapulapu was posted, and which sloped to the water's edge. As he advanced, the rebel chief himself, a man of gigantic stature, and decked out with brilliant feathers and paint, appeared at the brow of the hill, making defiant gestures at Magellan, and exhorting his followers to hold fast to their position.

An open strand was soon reached; and now the Spaniards stood, in close, resolute ranks, on the smooth sand. Magellan did not lose a moment in hesitation or delay. Forming his soldiers, he at once marched forward towards the hill.

But Cilapulapu, who had at first evidently intended to await the assault of his foe, changed his mind at the last moment; for no sooner did he see Magellan approaching the hill than, brandishing his spear, and giving a loud, fierce whoop, he rushed down the slope, followed by his forces. They were not less than fifteen hundred, against forty-nine; and as they descended, Magellan perceived that they were divided into three bodies. He had no time to note anything further, for in another moment they were close upon him. As they came on, they made a horrible noise with their shrieking and shouting, and leaped about like so many lunatics. Two of their companies separated to the right and left, with the intent to attack the Spaniards on their flanks; while the third advanced directly in their front. Magellan, dividing his little group into two companies, continued to go forward to meet his savage foes. He knew no fear, and at this critical moment he felt all the wild thrill of conflict. Then halting, he ordered his musketrymen and crossbowmen to fire.

Unhappily, neither bullets nor arrows seemed to take serious effect. The bullets, for the most part, whizzed harmlessly over the heads of the barbarians; while the arrows struck against the wooden shields, or passing through them, inflicted but slight wounds. At first, when the Spaniards opened fire upon them, the rebels paused in their headlong career, as if stunned by the noise of the volley, and to see what effect it would have. But when they perceived their ranks still un-broken, and but one or two of their comrades lying on the ground, they pressed forward more fiercely, and with more hideous screams than before.

Their arrows, javelins, spears, and stones, now fell like a hailstorm upon the Spaniards; and they found themselves, of a sudden, very hard pressed. With difficulty they avoided the deadly points of the savage weapons; they could scarcely hold their ground long enough to load and fire. It was clear that it must soon come to a hand-to hand fight.

Cilapulapu soon easily distinguished the daunt-less leader of his foes. Magellan's finer dress marked him out; his air of command betrayed him; and his intrepid valor, as he fought at the very head of his men, aroused the barbaric chief's wrath to its fiercest pitch. He ordered his men to aim at the Spanish captain their heaviest and deadliest javelins; and it was a miracle that Ma-gellan was not instantly overwhelmed by them.

At this moment Magellan perceived, for the first time, that his men were quite near some of the native huts. He ordered them to set fire to these; and soon ten or twelve of the huts were in a blaze. This redoubled the fury of the bar-barians, a number of whom rushed towards the men who had caused the conflagration and frantically assailed them. Two of the Spaniards fell, pierced by the javelins. The others made all haste to rejoin the main body of their comrades.

Cilapulapu, seeing that while the bodies of the Spaniards were effectually protected by their shields, but that their legs were exposed, ordered his troops to aim low. The savages now swarmed on all sides of the Spaniards, and hurled perfect avalanches of arrows and spears upon them. Magellan had hoped to use the cannon which he had brought in the boats; but, besides that the boats were obliged to anchor out of range of the enemy, it would now have been impossi-ble to fire the cannon without endangering his own men, as well as those of the Matan chief.

Magellan and his men were soon at close quarters with the furious host of savages; he himself was still the foremost, fighting with lion-like
and desperate valor. Lame as he was, he had
herculean strength in his arms; he dealt crushing
blows right and left with his long sword, and
native after native fell howling and dying beneath
them.

It was not long, however, before the over-
whelming numbers of the natives began to tell.
They fairly crowded the Spaniards back by their
very multitude. The Spaniards were forced to
retire towards the shore, fighting as they
went, and retreating as slowly as possible.

Of a sudden, Magellan fell to the earth with
a cry of pain; but before his soldiers could assist him, he was on his feet again. A poisoned
arrow had entered his left leg. He stooped and
pulled it out, and launched it back at the on-
rushing foe; and his sword continued to do as
sanguinary service as before. The natives had
now come near enough to use the arms they had
already hurled, over again. They picked up the
spears and arrows that lay strewn on the ground
where the Spaniards had stood, and again rained

them down upon their adversaries. Twice Magellan's helmet was knocked off his head; but fortunately his head itself was left unscathed. As coolly as if he had been standing on the deck of his flag-ship, he bent down each time, picked up his helmet, fastened it in its place, and went on fighting.

For more than an hour this terrific battle raged with unabating fury. Once more the Spaniards had made a desperate rally, and grimly resolved to stand to their ground at all hazards. They huddled close together, so as to face the enemy on each side; now and then a Spaniard would fall and writhe in agony, when a poisoned shaft entered and tortured his flesh; but for every Spaniard that fell, at least a half-a-dozen natives were laid low. The contest now raged at the very water's edge; and every moment a splash would be heard, and a dusky warrior would sink beneath the water.

The strength of the Spaniards was, all this while, slowly but surely giving out. It was evident that defeat and death stared them in the face. But their valor knew no shrinking, and even those whose blood streamed over their faces, and from the wounds in their arms and legs, fought doggedly on.

At last, however, a fatal event occurred, which speedily decided the conflict in favor of the bar. baric Cilapulapu. As Magellan was standing in front of his men, vigorously cutting and slashing on either side of him, a native rushed up and plunged a lance full in his face. The blood at once gushed from the wound, and covered the heroic Admiral's cheeks; but he rushed forward, seized his assailant's lance, and plunged it through his body, so that the point emerged from the other side. At this moment Magellan received another javelin wound in his right arm. He tried to pull the lance out of his foe's body, but, from the weakness of his arm, failed to do so; he then made an attempt to raise his sword, but found himself too weak. He staggered, and was about to fall, when an enormous savage, raising aloft a large scimetar, brought it with deadly force upon his left leg. Magellan sank down upon his face; and now a multitude of infuriated savages fell upon him. They ran him through and through with their spears and lances, and crushed his head in with stones; and without a word or a groan,

Death of Magellan. — Page 202.

the great discoverer and warrior breathed his last.

When the Spanish soldiers saw Magellan stretched upon the ground, all but seven or eight of the most valiant ran into the water, and hastened out towards the boats. The little band that remained continued to struggle desperately, but it was of no avail; and some of them found noble deaths within a few feet of the lifeless form of their brave chief.

Those who escaped into the water succeeded in reaching the boats in safety. The men who had remained in charge of them were overcome with grief to hear of the death of Magellan; they wept bitterly at the news, and vowed vengeance upon the barbarians who had thus deprived them of their commander. The boats drew up in a line alongside of each other, and the victorious savages having now poured down upon the shore, and some of them having even ventured into the water, the cannon were loaded and fired at them. Repeated volleys, issuing from the hoarse throats of the big guns, awoke the echoes; while the lesser volleys of the men's muskets aided them in their havoc. Many of the natives fell shrieking into the water; the rest retreated to the land, and to a secure distance beyond range of the cannon

It was useless for the boats to remain any longer at Matan. The enemy were in too formidable numbers, even if the boats of the king himself, which had been moored all this time about a mile off, in the rear, had joined those of the Spaniards in a new attack. The latter, therefore, slowly and mournfully pulled back to where the king was, and apprized him of the irreparable loss they had sustained. The sable monarch, on hearing it, threw himself back, raised his hands heavenward, and then, leaning forward on his knees, rocked to and fro, crying and moaning. The Spaniards were soon to learn how sincere this show of sorrow was.

The surprise and grief of the captains and crews of the fleet, at the intelligence brought by the boats, can scarcely be described. It was a dismal, dreary day for every soul on board. The wanderers were now without a guide; they had been deprived of him who had won their absolute trust, upon whose wisdom and courage they had surely counted, who had shared their every hardship, and had won the love of all, since the mutiny, by his kindness, his leniency towards their faults, his cheering words when they had been discouraged, and his fatherly care for the humblest of them.

Thus died the brave-souled, great-hearted, and indomitable Fernan Magellan, on Saturday, April 17th, 1521, at the early age of forty-one. Rarely has a more generous and noble character appeared in the pages of history. Magellan, after having braved mighty tempests, having undergone every danger of the sea, having resolutely pursued his purpose in spite of all obstacles, having with firm and stern hand put down the revolt of Carthagena, and having discovered the world-renowned straits, and crossed and given its name to the Pacific, was not destined to fulfil that other ambition of his, to make the circuit of the globe. He was fated to fall in the midst of his great voyage, a victim to the fury of savages, in defence of a potentate who had been friendly to him, and had consented to become a Christian. But, dying even at his early age, Magellan had done enough to win for his name immortal renown. He had at least shown the way around the world; so that from his time, the ships of all nations might follow in his track, and pass from nation to nation, in both hemispheres, by water.

We have seen how, under every circumstance, he was heroic and valiant in his action and bearing. He knew not fear, either of men or of the elements; was constant to his end in the worst fortunes, and never once despaired of achieving it. He did not falter when death and famine stared him in the face. He was loyal to his adopted sovereign, to his comrades, and himself.

Unlike Pizarro, and many other voyagers of his time, his ambition was a nobler one than that of the greed of gain; nor was it confined to winning fame and honor for himself. He aspired to confer great benefits upon man. He exulted in the thought that he might serve Christianity and civilization. He would find unknown pathways on the seas; he would plant the cross in heathen and idolatrous lands; and these high and unselfish aims he pursued with an ardor and intrepidity not surpassed by any of the world's conquerers and heroes.

Magellan was not wantonly cruel. He was never known to deal harshly with the innocent. To suppress the mutiny of St. Julian, to execute its ring-leaders, were acts of sheer necessity and self-preservation; but the mutiny subdued and its chiefs executed, he was mild and lenient with their misguided followers. Towards his sailors he was indulgent, generous, and considerate. He cheerfully shared their hardships. He tenderly cared for the sick. He overlooked their lighter faults; he was loth to punish even their more serious offences. He even gave the savage Cila-pulapu a chance to repent, before attacking him. He was kind and generous to all, high and low, alike. No man was more deeply beloved by his friends and his inferiors.

The achievement by which he is best known, and which has perpetuated his name, was the discovery of the Straits, that labyrinthine, dangerous passage between the southernmost point in South America and Terra del Fuego. Even now, it is not the safest thing in the world for a ship to steer its way through it; how much more difficult, when its outlet was unknown, and when the navigator had only the clumsy nautical contrivances of three centuries ago!

> "Forever sacred to the hero's fame,
> These foaming straits shall bear his deathless name."

CHAPTER XIV.

THE KING'S TREACHERY.

WITH the death of their brave commander, new troubles came upon the Spaniards. For awhile, all was confusion in the fleet. There was now no head; and it became necessary to replace Magellan by a new admiral. Two of the captains seemed, above all the other officers, best fitted to succeed to this office. One was Juan Serrano, who had proved not only a courageous and resolute man, but an able navigator, and a faithful friend of Magellan. The other was Edward Barbosa, a Portuguese, the brother of Magellan's wife, and the man whom, beyond all the rest in the fleet, Magellan had most thoroughly trusted.

The choice at last fell upon Barbosa; and no sooner had he received the command of the fleet, than he won the allegiance and confidence alike

of the sailors and of the officers. His first purpose was to secure, if possible, the remains of
Magellan, that the dead hero might be buried
with all honor, and his grave consecrated by the
rites of the Church. The king of Sebu, who
seemed overwhelmed by his friend's death, willingly agreed to make the attempt to recover his
body. He sent a boat with envoys to Matan,
who implored Cilapulapu to deliver it up; at the
same time promising that if he would do so, he
should have as much merchandize as he chose to
take.

Cilapulapu promptly made an insolent reply.
"He would on no account," he said, "give up
the body; he desired to keep it as a monument
of his triumph."

Barbosa was therefore obliged, with sad reluct-
ance, to abandon the hope of burying Magellan
in a manner worthy of his rank and character;
and now there seemed to be no reason why the
fleet should longer tarry at Sebu. Barbosa was
anxious to reach the long-wished-for Moluccas,
which, he knew, were not far off; and then to
sail home, as quickly as possible, by the way of
the Cape of Good Hope.

He ordered the goods which still lay in the
warehouse at Sebu, to be brought on board the
ships as quietly as possible ; and so skilfully was
this done, that the king of Sebu did not suspect
what was really going on.

Various incidents, indeed, had now happened,
which made Barbosa suspect the king's sincerity.
He knew that, immediately after Magellan's defeat and death, Cilapulapu had sent the king a
defiant message, threatening to invade Sebu
with an invincible force, if he did not at once
break with the Spaniards, and renounce Christianity. Barbosa saw that this threat had greatly
terrified the king, and had induced him to assume
a less cordial manner towards the fleet ; still, he
was profuse in his expressions of friendship, and
was far from offering the Spaniards any open
affront.

It seemed prudent to Barbosa, therefore, that
the fleet should set sail suddenly, before the king
knew that it was going, and before he could serve
the Spaniards, if such was really his disposition,
an ill turn.

Before he could put his project into execution,
it was foiled by the treachery of a man who had

hitherto been fidelity itself. This was the Malay interpreter, whom the Spaniards had named Henry. As soon as he had learned of Magellan's death, Henry had seemed overwhelmed with grief. He would go off to the further end of the flag-ship, wrap himself up in his mat, rock himself to and fro, and refuse all consolation. Barbosa allowed him to indulge his grief for awhile. But time was precious, and the Malay's assistance was absolutely necessary in getting the goods on board. Barbosa therefore spoke to him gently, and told him he must go on shore with the men. Henry would not stir, upon which Barbosa addressed him more roughly.

"You must know," said he, "that you are not free, though your master is dead. I am going to carry you to Spain, and deliver you to Doña Beatrix, the Admiral's widow. Meanwhile, if you do not get up quickly, and go ashore to your work, I will have you flogged."

The Malay upon this slowly rose, and walked sullenly away; he leaped into one of the boats and went ashore. He was very angry in his heart at Barbosa's threatening words, and resolved to be revenged on him. Slipping away from the rest,

while they were usy getting out the goods, he
hid himself in the thicket, and soon made his
way to the mansion of the king. To him he im-
parted the news that the ships were preparing to
set sail; and he urged the king to make haste
and attack them, so that he might get possession
both of the ships and their cargoes. The king
listened intently to what the treacherous Malay
said, and made up his mind to betray his guests.
He was all the more willing to do this, as he had
fully resolved to give up Christianity, and to make
peace with his rebellious subjects in Matan.
The Malay then returned to help the sailors, saying nothing, of course, of his visit to the king.

The next day, Barbosa received a message from
the king, that the jewels he designed as a present
to the king of Spain were ready to be delivered
to him; and inviting Barbosa with a number of
his principal officers and comrades, to dine with
him that afternoon.

Barbosa, though he had some suspicions of the
king, determined to accept the invitation. With
twenty-four others, among whom were an astrologer named San Martin, Carvalho, the chief of
police, and the Captain Serrano, and all of whom

took care to go armed to the teeth, he proceeded on shore at the appointed time.

The king met them in the open space, with many smiles and grimaces of welcome, and taking Barbosa by the hand, led him into the house. The other Spaniards, with a host of native courtiers and soldiers, followed. At the table, which was bountifully spread, Barbosa was seated at the king's right hand, a custom taught the natives by Magellan.

For a time the feast went on merrily. Barbosa and his comrades, who, on first coming, had taken care to be on their guard, and had cautiously watched every movement of the royal attendants seemed at last to forget their suspicions, and gave themselves wholly up to the good cheer of the occasion. While they were thus absorbed in the good things, the king of a sudden sprang from his seat, and making a signal to his soldiers, plunged a dagger deep into Barbosa's breast. At the same moment, each Spaniard was ferociously assailed by his dusky neighbors, and fell bleeding and dying at the foot of the festive board. The surprise and slaughter were as sudden as they were dastardly. Only one of the party—Serrano—escaped for the moment the fate of his brave comrades. He succeeded in felling two of his assailants, and leaping over their bodies, jumped to the ground, and ran, wounded and bleeding, through the open space down towards the shore.

But the swifter feet of the enraged natives caught up with him, just as he reached the strand, and was screaming to the ships for help with outstretched arms. The men on board looked at him in speechless terror and amazement. Meanwhile the savages caught him, bound him, and dragged him some distance along the shore. They offered the Spaniards to release Serrano, if they would give up two cannon, but it is probable that their offer was not heard; for in all haste the ships weighed anchor, and were soon scudding out of the bay. Serrano, as he saw his only hope thus vanishing, fell upon the ground with a shriek of despair, and was soon stabbed to death by the javelin and dagger-thrusts of his bloodthirsty captors.

After this barbarous and dastardly deed, the king of Sebu was only too ready to desert his Christian professions, and to make peace with

Cilapulapu. All his subjects, as well, speedily returned to their idols; and the little wooden figure of Christ was, as we have seen, afterwards used as a native deity. The cross which Magellan had set up was pulled down and burned.

Meanwhile, the fleet sailed away as fast as possible from the island where its occupants had witnessed so sudden a change from boundless hospitality to the most treacherous cruelty. Barbosa was dead; and in his place, one of the Spanish lieutenants, named Espinosa, was chosen admiral, and commander of the "Trinidad." Serrano's post of captain was given to Sebastian del Cano, who took command of the "Victoria."

Espinosa resolved not to turn back, but to still pursue the course which Magellan had marked out. The crews were reduced by battle, massacre, and illness, and they could hope neither to cope successfully with the perfidious king of Sebu, nor to conduct the ships back to Europe by way of the Straits of Magellan. Even now, they found it difficult to manage, in the gentle waters of the Archipelago, the three vessels which still remained to them.

When, therefore, the fleet reached an island called Bohol, about forty miles from Matan, they put in at an inviting harbor, in order to settle upon future plans. Espinosa made up his mind that one of the ships must be sacrificed; and as the "Conception" was the weakest and least sea-worthy of the three, she was doomed. Her cargo was transferred to the other ships, and she was then hauled up and burned.

The two vessels that remained, the "Trinidad" and the "Victoria," soon proceeded on their way. They sailed southwestward, in which direction Espinosa knew the Moluccas lay, and passed many islands without stopping. On one of these, they observed, the inhabitants were as black as Ethiopians, and their appearance was too forbidding to encourage the wanderers to land. After sailing a few days, they reached a much more hospitable-looking island, where the ships put in for wood and water. The king of the tribe went fearlessly on board the "Trinidad," and, as a token of his friendly disposition, drew some blood from his left hand, and smeared his face, breast, and the tip of his tongue with it. The Spaniards thought it prudent to follow his example, which they did rather awkwardly; but it pleased the dusky monarch very much. Espinosa, indeed, found this king so hospitable, that he resolved to prolong his stay. The ships entered the mouth of the river, which flowed from the hills of what proved to be one of the most beautiful islands the Spaniards had yet seen. This was Mindanao. The captains and sailors went freely on shore, and as soon as they did so the king and his courtiers began to sing and caper about, and offered them a very tempting meal of freshly-caught fish.

So much confidence did the king inspire in Espinosa and the other officers, that they were easily persuaded to visit him in the town. It was a rash thing to do, considering the base treatment to which they had just been subjected by the king of Sebu; but that perfidy seems to have been so soon forgotten. Espinosa and his comrades did not neglect, however, to arm themselves, so as to be fully prepared for foul play. The town lay for the most part on the bank of the river, from which it straggled up a gentle slope, wooded with palms and many other tropical trees.

It was night when Espinosa and his party as
cended the hill, in company with the sable king
and his retinue; and as they approached its
crest, a large number of the natives came to
meet them with blazing torches, which lit up the
scene with a wierd, lurid glare. The figures of
the natives looked almost terrible in the flicker.
ing and fitful light, their painted faces and dark,
unclothed forms standing out against the dark.
ness.

The king conducted his visitors within the long,
low hut which constituted his palace; and the first
thing he did was to feast them. In the principal
apartment, the Spaniards found two ravishingly
beautiful women, with almost fair complexions,
and exquisite forms and features, who proved to
be two of his majesty's wives; two of the chiefs
attended the king inside the hut; and the king,
his wives, and the chiefs began at once to quaff
long draughts of palm wine from enormous
wooden goblets. Espinosa was prevailed on
to imitate their example; but Pigafetta, the
Italian, who was of the party, thought it pru.
dent only to sip the strong liquor. Supper fol.
lowed, consisting mainly of very salt fish, served

up in porcelain dishes, and of rice very much
boiled.

The party from the fleet remained one night
in the king's house; and the next morning they
breakfasted with him, as cozily as possible, the
food being the same as on the night before,
Pigafetta, who no longer had the least fear of
the king or his subjects, took a stroll after break-
fast over the island. He found it full of mar-
vels of vegetable and floral beauty, and resplend-
ent with all the rich and varied growths of the
tropics. On reaching the summit of a hill, hard
by that on which the king's house stood, he found
another large mansion, which, he was told by the
natives who went with him, was the residence of
one of the queens. He found no difficulty in
gaining admission, and was cordially welcomed
by its fair occupant, who was weaving a mat,
and who made him sit beside her. She was surrounded by a number of male and female slaves,
and there were many porcelain ornaments and
musical instruments hanging from the walls.
Before Pigafetta departed, the queen amused him
by playing very loudly on some metal timbrels.

He was returning towards the ships, when he

was met by several of the chiefs, who offered to row him down the river in a long canoe. This offer he smilingly accepted. As they sped smoothly down the stream, he saw on the shore the bodies of three men hanging upon a tree. On asking what this meant, he was told that they were thieves, and that this was the way that such criminals were punished in Mindanao. He also saw, on the banks, and in the fields that he passed in the canoe, many pigs, goats, and fowl of various breeds.

What surprised and dazzled Pigafetta still more, was the abundance of gold ornaments which the natives displayed. Some of the utensils in the king's house were of this precious metal; the queen had many gold rings and bracelets; and gold seemed to be a common article, even with the natives. The chiefs in the canoe, as they passed along, pointed out several valleys to Pigafetta, telling him by signs that they contained many rich veins of gold; but that as they had no iron implements with which to mine it, they could only procure it with labor and difficulty.

Refreshed by their pleasant sojourn at Min-

danao, the wanderers resumed their voyage, con-
tinuing to pass, as before, many islands, some of
which seemed deserted, and others inhabited by
Malay tribes. They sailed perhaps a hundred
miles in a westerly direction, until they reached
an island called Palawan.

The provisions of the ships were now pretty
much exhausted; and Espinosa, for some unex-
plained reason, had neglected to replenish his
stores at Mindanao. Before reaching Palawan,
the men had been put on short rations. It was,
therefore, much to their relief that they saw
another large and fruitful island rising from the
sea; and still greater was their delight to find
the people of Palawan and their rulers as hospitable and well-disposed as those of the place
they had recently left.

The king was a very tall and imposing-looking
man, whose countenance, when he first appeared,
so dark was it, and so long and black his beard,
seemed forbidding. But on going on board the
flag-ship, his face was lit up with a smile so
beaming and pleasant, and he seemed so sin-
cerely rejoiced to see the strangers, that Espinosa
and his comrades were at once put at their ease.

Palawan proved to be and to contain all that the Spaniards hoped. The king was generous, his people were peaceable and good-natured, and the island abounded in good things. They found not only pigs and goats, but yams (like our sweet potatoes), large and luscious bananas, and, of course, plenty of rice, cocoanuts, and sugar-canes. The pigs were cured and stowed away for future use; meanwhile the Spaniards feasted daily and freely with their new friends.

The natives seemed more civilized and intelligent than those of the other islands. They had a great fondness for gay colors and jewelry; and were wild with joy when Espinosa gave them some little brass bells, which they hung on their fingers and ears, and danced about to hear them jingle.

They had, it appeared, a superstitious respect for cocks, which they reared with great care, and never ate; but on festival days brought them out and made them fight each other. To one of these cock-fights Espinosa and his officers were invited.

A week was passed at Palawan, during which the ships were repaired (a task in which the na tives willingly helped the carpenters), provisions in plenty were stored, and wood and water were put in ; and when the strangers departed, the king, with a great number of his subjects, embarked in a large fleet of long canoes, and attended the "Trinidad" and the "Victoria" far out to sea.

CHAPTER XV.

ADVENTURES AT BORNEO.

THE ships had not sailed southwestward more than thirty miles, when Espinosa, standing on the deck of the " Trinidad," which was ahead of the "Victoria," espied an island longer, and yet wilder and more luxuriant in its foliage and vegetation than any he had before seen. It was a bright, glowing morning in summer, and the tropical air was heavy with the perfume of fruit and flower, as a gentle breeze blew off the land towards the ships.

As the island was neared, however, Espinosa, who resolved to land if circumstance favored it, saw no harbor where to enter. The shores rose in high and abrupt bluffs ; and in places where there were bays or inlets, the water near the shore proved so full of rocks that to approach any of them would have been dangerous. So he skirted the coast of the island all that day, and a part of the next; and was surprised at its extent and at all he saw on the shore. Now and then groups of natives appeared on the bluffs, of a more dusky hue and wilder appearance than those at Palawan; but they did not seem afraid of the ships, gazing at them rather with curiosity than with terror or hostility.

About noon on the second day, Espinosa at last caught sight of a good harbor, beyond which the cliffs jutted far into the sea. The harbor was evidently at the mouth of a river; and on the banks of this was to be seen a large and prosperous-looking town. The island indeed, was Borneo, and the town its capital, Bruni. Bruni was situated on the northwest coast.

Espinosa, who had grown bold and confident by the good treatment he had received since leaving Sebu, did not hesitate to enter the port, and to anchor his ships in a favorable place, quite near the shore. The natives crowded along the beach, but their demonstrations were not at all unfriendly. They acted as if European ships were not a wholly unwonted sight to them, but as if they were not so new as to have ceased to be an attractive sight.

That night the Spaniards remained quietly in their ships, mounting guard, of course, lest by any chance the islanders should prove hostile. No incident, however, disturbed the quiet of the dark hours; and officers and crews slept soundly.

The morning was not far advanced, when Espinosa saw a very handsome barge, its prow and stern glittering with gilt, and a white and blue flag fluttering from the bow, push out from the beach and approach the "Trinidad." The barge was full of gaily-dressed natives, with very dark skins and shaggy hair, who were playing upon pipes and drums. After the barge came several smaller boats, which appeared to be fishing smacks. The barge presently came alongside; and, without more ado, eight of its occupants, old men with bushy white heads, clambered upon the deck of the flag-ship. They were chiefs of the island; and were followed by their attendants, who brought on board a variety of gifts for the strangers.

Espinosa received them with great politeness, and offered them seats on a carpet that was spread upon the deck, which they accepted with grave and stately courtesy. Then they caused their attendants to spread before the Spaniards the good things they had brought. There were large wooden vessels, gorgeously painted, and filled with betel, the fruit they constantly chewed in that part of the world; there were jars of arrack, a curious beverage, which the Spaniards found very palatable, but quite strong, and which, they learned, was made from rice; there were, besides, fowl and goats, sugar-cane and bananas.

After paying a visit to the flag-ship, the chiefs went on board the "Victoria," whither they carried similar gifts, and met with an equally hearty welcome. It was not long before their good treatment had its effect on the king of Borneo. He sent three barges, yet more splendid than that which had first appeared, full of chiefs and musicians, who were rowed around the ships, the musicians playing with all their might. Espinosa ordered salutes to be fired, and the flags to be hoisted at the mast-heads. Among other articles that the natives brought, as gifts from their monarch, were cakes made of rice, honey and eggs; all of which were extremely welcome to the Spaniards, who eagerly consumed them.

The king of Borneo, a day or two after, sent a message that the Spaniards might not only procure such provisions as they wished on shore, but that they might trade freely with his subjects.

Espinosa ordered seven of his principal men, one of whom was Pigafetta, to get into one of the barges, go to the town, and visit the king. These carried with them, as friendly offerings, a Turkish coat of green velvet, a chair of violet-colored velvet, some red cloth, a cap, a gilt goblet, a glass vase, and, oddly enough, a gilt pen and ink case; and, to be given to the queen, a pair of slippers, and a silver case full of pins. Presents were also carried for the king's chief courtiers; for Espinosa rightly judged that it was of no small importance to gain the friendship of a potentate evidently so rich and powerful.

When the party reached the quay and disembarked, they were forced to wait some time; for the king had not understood that they were coming, and had not made his preparations to receive them.

At last, however, a sight greeted their eyes

The Reception at Borneo. — Page 228.

which gave them a still higher idea of the royal
splendor of Borneo. Two immense elephants,
caparisoned in rich and vari-colored silk, came
slowly tramping down to the quay. With them
were twelve natives, all richly dressed, and bearing large porcelain vases covered with silk nap-
kins. These vases, it appeared, were intended to
receive the presents which the Spaniards had
brought with them. The elephants were supplied
with palanquins on which could be seated quite
a number of men; and the Spaniards clambered
up to them on the shoulders of the natives.

The elephants were then slowly led through
the streets of the town, which was a far handsomer and more spacious place than any the
Spaniards had hitherto seen in the islands. As
they went along, the people, who were of a
higher type of men and women than those before visited, gathered in curious crowds, and
lined the sides of the streets. They were quiet,
though Pigafetta saw many fierce and savage-
looking faces among them.

Pigafetta and his comrades were conducted to
the house of one of the most important men,
where, it being now nearly dark, they were invited

to enter, and stay over-night. They found everything in the house much more elegant and comfortable than in the houses at Sebu. Instead of
coarse mats, they had soft cotton rugs to sleep
on; and the viands set before them were very
pleasant and palatable.

The next morning the elephants were again
awaiting them at the door; and they mounted
the palanquins, and set out for the royal palace,
the men who bore the presents going before them.
The palace they found to be a large and rather
imposing edifice, the hall of which was reached
by a broad flight of steps. On entering the hall,
Pigafetta was amazed at its aspect of show and
ceremony. It was hung with brilliant silks, and
was full of the dusky courtiers in fine clothes.
Beyond this apartment was another, not quite
so spacious, but raised a few feet higher, and
reached by a short flight of steps; it was
very richly hung with long curtains of silk and
brocade, and two large windows admitted the
light. Here were stationed three hundred of the
king's guard, with daggers drawn. Yet beyond
this room was a third, much smaller, but more
splendidly adorned; and here sat the king, a

rather fat man, forty years old, on a great cush-
ion, with one of his little boys. The king was
busily chewing the eternal betel.

Surrounding the king was a bevy of women of
various complexions, some almost as light as
Europeans, others dark enough to have come
from Africa.

The visitors were not allowed to approach
nearer the monarch than the first hall. There
they were supplied with cushions, so placed that
they could see the king in the distance. When
they were seated they were given to understand
that they could not themselves speak to his
majesty; but that, whatever they had to say to
him, they must say to a certain chief; this chief
would tell it to another, who would repeat it to a
yet higher official; who, in his turn, would deliver
the message through a speaking-trumpet to the
prime minister, who stood at the king's side, and
by whom it would at last reach the royal ears.

At the same time, the chief who gave them
these instructions, told them they must rise, join
their hands above their heads, raise first one and
then the other foot, make three low bows to the
king, and then kiss their hands to him.

This Pigafetta and his comrades did with great care and punctiliousness; being not a little amused to find, in this semi-barbarous and pagan court, quite as much ceremony as in the palaces of refined Europe.

They then, in the indirect manner that has been described, made known to the royal host the message which Espinosa had sent. It was, that they were subjects of the king of Spain, who wished to establish peace and friendship with the king of Borneo, and for permission to trade with the island. The next thing was to offer the king the presents they had brought; which were accordingly laid at his feet by some of his attendants. He acknowledged them by a slight and solemn inclination of the head; and immediately after sent to the Spaniards some pieces of rick silk and brocade.

They were next treated to cloves and cinnamon; and while they were eating, the curtains in front of the king were drawn together, and he disappeared from view. Pigaffetta observed, on this occasion, that the soldiers and courtiers wore cloth of gold and silk, that their daggers had gold hilts studded with gems, and that their fingers were fairly covered with large rings.

Deeply impressed with all that they had seen, the party returned to the house of the chief where they had lodged, mounted, as when they came, upon elephants. There they were once more entertained in the most lavish manner. The hospitable chief feasted them upon rice, chickens, and peacocks, veal, many kinds of fish, and the not unpleasant arrack; these things, too, were served to them on handsome china dishes. The Spaniards were obliged to eat with their fingers; but the rice they ate with gold spoons, to find which, in Borneo, much surprised them.

They remained two days in the chief's abode; and on the second night were provided not only with wax candles, but even with oil lamps. Everything they saw, indeed, astonished them at the evident riches and even civilization of the island.

When Pigafetta reported the adventures of his party to the Admiral, he was more than ever convinced that it was important to secure the king's good will for the Spaniards. Espinosa was impatient to reach the Moluccas; but was so attracted by all that he had seen and heard in Borneo that he made up his mind to prolong his stay. Instead of a sojourn of two or three days, therefore, the ships remained anchored in the harbor nearly a month.

Espinosa himself, as well as his officers and men, now went freely to and fro, every day, between the ships and the town. The king's barges were always ready to conduct them, and the houses of the chiefs were always at their disposal. Espinosa desired the monarch to visit the ships; but was told that he never stirred away from his palace, except when he went hunting, which he occasionally did with a few chosen princes and nobles.

The Spaniards availed themselves of the kindly disposition of the people to open trade with them. They secured a warehouse near the quay; and here, as at Sebu, a brisk business soon sprang up. The people of Borneo, it turned out, knew much better the value of the articles offered for sale by the Spaniards, than those of Sebu; and Espinosa's men found it necessary to display the best articles the ships afforded.

Something new about Borneo and its people was learned every day. Espinosa estimated the population of the town at nearly one hundred thousand. A large part of it was built on piles driven in the water; the houses were all of wood, and were reached by flights of steps. In front of the royal palace was a thick and high brick wall, with port-holes. This was intended as a kind of fort to protect the king.

Espinosa soon learned that the people of Borneo were not idolaters, but were faithful followers of Mahomet; and that they scrupulously obeyed the precepts of the Koran. They never ate pig's flesh, nor the flesh of any animal they did not themselves kill. The mass of the people went almost naked, as, indeed, the hot climate in which they lived made it almost necessary to do; but the nobles and soldiers, as we have seen, dressed very gaily.

Their money was not unlike the European. It consisted of bronze coins, pierced in the centre for stringing together; and, as Espinosa and his companions were able to see for themselves, the natives were very skilful in making fine porcelain and china. Among the productions of the island

were camphor, cinnamon, ginger, oranges, lemons, melons, cucumbers, cabbage, onions, and
sugar-canes; their animals were elephants, horses,
pigs, goats, fowl, and geese. The medicine they
thought the most effective was quick-silver, which
they were bold enough to swallow when ill.

The king, it appeared, was very rich. Many
of his household utensils were of solid gold;
some of his plates and covers were artistically
enamelled and chased. Some of the Spaniards,
on going one day to the palace, were shown two
enormous and beautiful pearls, nearly as large as
hen's eggs. They were told that the king had
bought these pearls from the Arabs, for a vast
sum, and that he esteemed them his most precious treasure.

Early one morning, shortly before the day set
for the departure of the ships from Borneo,
Espinosa was awakened to hear some startling
news. The king and people had treated him so
kindly and generously, that he had long ceased
to have the slightest suspicion of their good
faith. What was his surprise and alarm, then,
when one of his officers, entering his cabin, exclaimed:

" Rise quickly, Admiral. There is a large fleet of junks coming towards us, full of armed men. Their design is without doubt a hostile one. Unless we prepare at once to resist them, we shall surely be overwhelmed!"

Espinosa arose, dressed himself with all speed, and ran up on deck. The sight which greeted his eyes only confirmed the officer's report. There, in the broad bay, which sparkled with the reflection of the first rays of the sun, was a fleet of native junks, with their bamboo masts and bark sails, of which there could not be less than a hundred. They were divided into three squadrons, and sailed together in close phalanx. Their decks were, indeed, fairly crowded with Borneo warriors, who presented a very formidable aspect. Espinosa at once made up his mind that it had been the intention of the king to take him by surprise ; and in this, if it was his purpose, he had quite succeeded. To resist so large and powerful a fleet would have been folly. With his handful of men, and his few cannon, Espinosa could not hope to make a serious impression upon it. He resolved to lose no time in weighing anchor and setting sail, so as to escape if possible, before it was too late. Meanwhile, he was beside himself with anger at what he supposed to be the unparalleled perfidy of the king of Borneo.

The order to weigh anchor was given, and the " Trinidad" and " Victoria" began to move. At this moment several junks, which had been lying just by the ships for several days, showed signs, as Espinosa thought, of following them. He ordered them to be fired upon with the cannon. The balls did deadly work. Two of the junks foundered, and two more went aground on a shoal, in trying to escape the attack; while a number of their occupants were killed.

Espinosa soon had reason to bitterly regret his haste in firing upon these junks. A smaller boat was seen rapidly approaching the flag-ship, showing a flag of truce. When it came up, Espinosa permitted a chief, who was standing up in the boat and eagerly waving his arms, to come on board.

All was then explained. It seemed that it was not at all the object of the large fleet of junks to attack the Spaniards. This armament was just returning from a warlike expedition to the island of Luzon, some leagues away, where the soldiers had been engaged in a fierce conflict with a powerful enemy of their sovereign. The chief city of the island had been sacked, and many prisoners and much booty taken.

The Admiral made all haste to return to his old anchorage in the harbor, and to make all the reparation he could for having attacked the junks and killed those who were in them. The king was easily persuaded of the error Espinosa had committed, and accepted his apologies and presents with cordial good will; and from that time until the ships sailed their relations continued to be of the most friendly nature. The ships received new supplies of provisions, wood, and water; and Espinosa found, on balancing his accounts, that the active trade with the towns-people had been quite profitable.

It was autumn when the "Victoria" and the "Trinidad," with flags flying and cannon bellowing forth their noisy farewells, at last sailed out of the hospitable harbor of Borneo, and proceeded on their way in search of the Moluccas.

CHAPTER XVI.

DISCOVERY OF THE SPICE ISLANDS.

ESPINOSA had learned that, in searching for the Moluccas, he had sailed too far westward; and on leaving Borneo he deemed it wisest to return on the track by which he had come, and to pass around the island of Borneo by the north and east. Scarcely were the ships fairly out to sea, when the Admiral discovered that they were both leaky, and sadly needed repairs; and he was obliged to look about for a convenient island to haul them over and caulk them. Seeing a place that seemed fit for this purpose, he approached it; but, as the "Victoria" was nearing the shore, she struck on some shoals, and came near being lost. She was got off, however, though with great difficulty.

About the same time the "Trinidad" came very near being blown up, with all on board. A sailor was snuffing a candle, and very incautiously threw the lighted wick into a chest of gunpowder which was standing near by. Quick as a flash he sprang, grasped and extinguished the wick. In another instant, a terrible explosion must have occurred.

Finally the ships found a harbor on an island called Cinbonbon, where the repairs might be made with great convenience; and here they cast anchor. On examining the ships more narrowly, Espinosa found that they were yet more unseaworthy than he had at first thought. It was necessary to take time to put them in thorough order again. He therefore resolved to remain at Cinbonbon, as long as was necessary for this purpose.

While the carpenters were busy with the ships, the sailors went on shore, and built little huts, where they could stay with more comfort than on ship-board. Cinbonbon, like nearly all the islands in the Archipelago, was very picturesque and fruitful. Some of the men were set to gathering wood in the forest, for the repairs on the ships; and this they found no easy matter, as the ground was fairly covered with briars and

thorny shrubs, and most of the men having no
shoes, were obliged to go among them bare-
foot.

Some amused themselves with hunting the
wild boars, which were plentiful and very savage
in the island; others went crocodile shooting;
others contented themselves with the gentle
sport of catching fish, oysters, and turtles, with
which to regale their comrades. These caught
many fish, the like of which they had never before seen; one had a head which resembled that
of a pig, and which had two horns. Pigafetta saw
with astonishment the leaves of a certain kind
of tree, which, when they fell to the ground,
moved about as if they were living things.
"I kept one," he said, "nine days in a box.
When I opened it, the leaf skipped round the box.
I believe they live upon air." The mystery of this
is, however, easily explained. If Pigafetta had examined his animated leaf a little more closely,
he would have seen that its motions came from
an insect which lived inside of it.

While the ships were at Cinbonbon, the sailors
captured a junk that was passing by, loaded with
cocoanuts, which they appropriated; allowing

the natives to escape as best they could among
the islands.

It was more than a month before the ships
were ready to sail for Cinbonbon. They then
continued their voyage northward and eastward, taking in Mindanao, where they had before
tarried. On their way, as they went, the Spaniards captured all the junks they could lay their
hands on, compelling them to give up their
cargoes, which in some cases consisted of rice,
pigs, goats, fowl, figs, sugar-canes, and palm
wine. They passed among many islands which
they had not before seen ; and at one of these
they obtained some cinnamon, of which they had
long been in search, and for which they willingly
exchanged some knives.

At last they reached a region where there were
more signs of thrift and commerce, where the
natives were tall, robust, and intelligent-looking
men, and where the vessels were larger and better made even than those of Borneo. Then
Espinosa felt sure that he was approaching the
far-famed Moluccas, or Spice Islands, which it
was one of the main objects of Magellan to find.
At one of the islands at which the ships stopped,

a chief told him that he knew where the Moluccas were; and he proceeded to describe the quarter in which they lay. Espinosa lost no time in following the directions given by this chief. He now took a southeast course, and made as much speed as the winds and current would permit.

The ships had not, however, gone far, when a furious tropical storm burst upon them, and for awhile threatened their destruction. For some days the Spaniards were overwhelmed with fear, lest they should be dashed upon the rocks of the islands and reefs that thickly studded the seas. When the tempest subsided a little they made all haste to seek shelter in a bay. It happened that, on the island where this bay was, there was a Malay familiar with the whole region of the Archipelago; and Espinosa was not long in persuading him, by means of presents, to undertake to pilot the ships to the Spice Islands.

It was a mild morning, early in November, when Espinosa, standing on the deck of the flagship, with the Malay pilot by his side, espied in the dim distance four islands, lying near together, all of which were very uneven and hilly.

The Malay, as soon as he caught sight of them, exclaimed that they were the Moluccas. The Admiral delighted to hear this, at once told the crew, and signalled the good news to the "Victoria," which was following at the distance of about a half-a-mile. The wanderers had been more than two years on their voyage; and were now to behold with their own eyes, the islands, the report of whose riches had dazzled all Europe. In their joy they fired the cannon, and made merry on the decks.

Espinosa only feared one thing. He had heard, in Spain, that these Spice Islands, which promised so much to their conqueror, were well-nigh inaccessible to ships. They were said to be surrounded with dangerous shoals, and to be usually enveloped in dark, dismal fogs. The islands now stood out distinct and bold, however, in an atmosphere which grew clearer as the morning advanced; and his anxiety ceased, when, on approaching the nearest, he found the water many fathoms deep, close up to the shore.

In the middle of the afternoon the ships entered a wide and fine harbor, and were able to cast anchor in twenty fathoms of water. On

the shore stood a town of prosperous and
civilized appearance; and along the bea ., and
the rocks that rose from the water's e jge on
either side, the natives were gathered in large
numbers, gazing curiously at the European vessels as they lay in the roadstead. The island
the Spaniards thus reached was one of the larger
Moluccas, and was called Tidor.

Early the next morning the sultan of the
island, whose name, as the Spaniards soon learned,
was Almansor, came out in a gorgeous barge,
and rowed around the two ships. When the
barge passed under the bows of the " Trinidad,"
Espinosa was able to perceive that the sultan
was of a cream-colored complexion, with a black
flowing beard, about forty-five years of age, well-
built, and strikingly handsome. He wore a fine
white tunic, the ends of the sleeves of which were
embroidered with gold lace; and a long skirt, or
robe, which fell to his feet. On his head he had
a thin silk veil, over which he wore a garland of
flowers. His appearance was very gay and picturesque. Above him was spread a silk umbrella,
to protect him from the sun.

Espinosa made all haste to welcome the sul

tan's friendly advances. He caused a long-boat
to be lowered, got into it, and rowed to the side
of the barge. The sultan smiled, stretched out
his hands, and beckoned pleasantly to the Admiral to come on board his vessel. This Espinosa did willingly and with alacrity.

He was invited to take a seat beside the monarch. On the other side sat the young prince,
the sultan's son, who held a long gold sceptre;
while in front of the sultan crouched two of his
attendants with gold ewers full of water, with
which the sultan moistened his fingers after taking betel, which two other attendants had ready
for him in gold boxes.

It appeared that the sultan was a Mohamme-
dan, and a man of no inferior intelligence. Espinosa had taken care to have an interpreter
with him; and through him he now entered into
conversation with his royal host.

"I long ago dreamed," said the sultan, "that
some ships were coming hither from distant
countries. I am an astrologer as well as a king,
and have examined the moon to see if this was
true; and the moon assured me it was so. And
now I see that the moon did not deceive me."

"We have come to offer you the friendship of our great sovereign, the king of Spain," replied Espinosa; "and to trade peaceably with your people; and I am very grateful to you for this kind reception."

"If you are true and sincere," returned the sultan, "you shall be welcome; and I shall receive and return your sovereign's friendship with delight."

Espinosa then invited the sultan to go on board the flag-ship. He consulted apart a few moments with several of his nobles, and then, turning to the Admiral, signified his willingness to comply with his proposal.

As the barge drew near the "Trinidad," the cannon bellowed forth their hoarse welcome; the flags were run up at the mast-heads; and the officers and sailors, gathering at the side of the deck, waved their hats and loudly cheered. Preparations to receive the monarch were hurriedly made; and when he had mounted the ladder, followed by some of his attendants and by Espinosa, he was conducted to a red velvet chair, which had been placed in the middle of the deck. Espinosa then advanced, and bowing low, threw over the royal shoulders a rich yellow velvet rug. Each Spaniard came forward and kissed the sultan's hand, and then sat down on the deck in front of him. He was regaled with wine and cakes, and appeared highly pleased with his reception. He declared to Espinosa that he was now quite sure of the good faith of the strangers; and as a proof of this, he gave full permission to them to go on shore as much as they pleased, and to use the houses of his subjects just as if they were their own.

Not content with this concession, the sovereign said that, in honor of the sovereign of his guests, his island should no longer be called Tidor, but Castile.

Before the sultan departed, Espinosa, who was most anxious to make sure of his good will, overwhelmed him with presents. He gave him the red velvet chair in which he had sat on the deck; he had a number of pieces of cloth. linen, brocade, and damask, brought, and laid at the royal feet; he begged him to accept some large mirrors, some glass beads, knives, scissors, combs, and goblets. To the young prince he was not less generous, presenting him with a fine cap, a robe of silk and gold, and a handsome mirror; while he lavished other gifts of knives, caps, and cloths upon the principal men of the sultan's retinue.

It may well be believed that the sultan and his people, after this, were fairly delighted with their visitors. As the sultan descended into his barge, ne called out to Espinosa to bring his ships yet closer to the shore; and told him that if any of the natives approached them at night, he might fire at them as much as he pleased. The departing barge was saluted with the cannon and the loud acclamations of the men; and that night Espinosa gave a bountiful supper to the officers of both ships, who made merry over their good fortune in finding the Moluccas, and in being so well received there.

The following days were employed much as the time had been when the ships were sojourning at Borneo. The men went on shore freely, and were regaled very hospitably in the town, and by the royal court. They opened a lively trade with the natives, their main object being to fill up their cargoes with spices; and they also took in an abundance of provisions of all kinds. The sultan grew every day more cordial in his professions and more hospitable in his conduct; and it was not long before he was ready to swear that Tidor and Tarenate, (a neighboring island) should be subject to the king of Spain, for whom he himself would "fight to the death," as his faithful vassal. Finding that the Spaniards were anxious to obtain a quantity of cloves, he went in person, in his barge, to one of the other islands, and brought back several loads of cloves for them.

Espinosa might have suspected that this sudden and profuse friendship could scarcely be sincere; but at first he had full faith in the sultan's good faith. He had not been long in Tidor, however, before events took place that put him on his guard, and caused him to hasten as much as possible the loading of his ships.

Some years before, it seemed, Francisco Serrano, a Portuguese voyager, and the friend of Magellan who had first put it into his head to make this expedition, had found the Moluccas by sailing round the Cape of Good Hope, and eastward from India. He had won the friendship of the king and natives of the isle of Tarenate, near Tidor; and had there established a Portuguese trade

station. The king of Tidor, who had long been
at war with the king of Tarenate, entertained a
violent hatred of the Portuguese; and Espinosa
heard that, on one occasion, when the king of
Tidor had conquered his enemy, he had caused
Serrano to be poisoned, and had killed all the
Portuguese he could lay his hands on. Meanwhile, the Portuguese trade station at Tarenate
was still in existence, at the time Espinosa came
to Tidor.

One day a fleet of barges appeared at the head
of the bay, sailing from the direction of the
island of Tarenate; and when they came within a
short distance of the ships, they cast anchor, and
sent a messenger on board the " Trinidad." From
him Espinosa learned that the prince of Tarenate, though an enemy of the king of Tidor, had
arrived to make peace and friendship with the
Spaniards, and desired to come on board the
flag-ship. Espinosa replied that he could not receive the prince without first obtaining the consent of the king of Tidor. This the king readily
granted; but now the prince grew suspicious,
and moved away from the ships. Espinosa
thereupon sent him some presents, and begged

that the Portuguese factor in Tarenate, Pedro de Lorosa, should come and visit the ships. A few days after Lorosa made his appearance. He told Epinosa that he had been in the Moluccas ten years, and that he had already heard of Magellan's expedition. He surprised the Admiral, moreover, by declaring that the king of Portugal, angry that Magellan had sailed in Spanish ships, had sent out a fleet by way of the Cape of Good Hope to contest his passage; but that this fleet had been compelled to turn back, on account of contrary winds.

Espinosa finally persuaded Lorosa to return to Spain with him; and they soon became fast friends. It was not long before Lorosa grew more confidential, and began to warn Espinosa against trusting too much to the sincerity of the king of Tidor. He related how the Portuguese had been assassinated, and expressed his suspicions that the Spaniards should meet the same fate unless a strict watch were kept.

Some things that happened about this time served to arouse Espinosa's fears of the king's intentions. The king wished to give a great feast to the officers and crews. Espinosa remembered

that it was by giving such a feast that the per.
fidious king of Sebu had decoyed the other cap.
tains into his house, only to murder them with.
out mercy; and prudently declined the invita.
tion. He saw, too, that the Tidor chiefs took
every chance they could get to whisper mysteri.
ously to the prisoners he had brought with him
from the other islands; and guessed that this was
for no good purpose.

Meanwhile, the Spaniards made excursions
among the other islands, and busied themselves
with completing their cargoes. In these excur.
sions they saw and heard many curious things,
a description of which we will reserve for another
chapter.

CHAPTER XVII.

SAILING TOWARDS HOME.

THE Spaniards found the other islands as beautiful and as fruitful as Tidor; and such was the fear with which they were regarded by the natives—for it was evidently their sense of the warlike superiority of the Spaniards, more than any love for them, that rendered these barbarians so submissive and friendly—that they were allowed to go freely into the houses, and to wander at will over the fields and through the forests.

Pigafetta, the inquisitive Italian who has been so often mentioned, seized the opportunity to observe everything in these strange islands with a curious eye. He was especially struck with the spice trees and shrubs, which yielded products so valuable in Europe; and one of his first excursions was to a grove of clove trees.

These he found to grow quite high, with trunks as thick as a man's body; and they only grew on high land. The branches spread out at the middle, and narrowed to the shape of a cone at the top. The bark was of an olive color, and the leaves much like those of the laurel. The cloves, he found, were white when they first appeared; they gradually deepened into red, and when dry became dark brown. Two crops were gathered each year; one at Christmas, and the other about the middle of June. The leaves, bark, and even the wood of the clove tree had the same perfume, he noticed, that the clove itself had. The natives told him that the cloves were ripened by the mountain mists; and must be gathered in the nick of time, or they would become so hard as to be useless.

He examined with equal curiosity the nutmeg trees, which reminded him of the walnut trees of Europe. The nutmegs, when gathered, were shaped like small quinces, and had a soft fur, or down, upon them. The outside rind was quite thick; beneath it was a thin, web-like covering: under this, a bright red bark, and within the bark the nut itself, as we see it in the market.

The ginger shrub did not escape Pigafetta's quick eye. He found that this shrub shot out of the ground in long branches like the shoots of canes, and that its leaves were like those of the cane. The ginger itself was, of course, the fragrant root of the shrub; in order to dry it, the natives used lime.

Many of the ways and customs of the people were interesting. It appeared that the bread they ate was made of the wood of a tree that somewhat resembled the palm. They took a piece of the wood and extracted certain long black thorns they found inclosed in it; these they pounded into a powder, and cooked it as we do flour. The bread thus made, however, did not seem to Pigafetta very palatable.

The king of Tidor had no less than two hundred wives, one only of whom was acknowledged as his queen. The others were inferior to her in rank. These wives all lived in a long mansion outside the town, where the king visited them when he chose. They were most carefully guarded; and if any man were found near their house, either at night or in the day-time, he was at once put to death. The king always ate alone,

or with his queen, on a raised platform, below
which the rest of his family were gathered. No
one else ate until his majesty had finished. Each
noble family was bound to provide the monarch
with a wife. The only other person who was
permitted to have a number of wives was a sort
of bishop, or high priest, whose rank was next to
the king. This holy personage had forty wives,
and more than a hundred children.

These islanders, like those of Mindanao, and
others the Spaniards had already visited, regarded the pig as a sort of sacred animal; and as
soon as the King of Tidor found that there were
pigs on board the ships, he begged the Admiral
that they should all be at once slaughtered, saying that he would fully make up for the loss with
fowl and goats. Espinosa humored him, and had
all the pigs killed, and hung up on deck, so that
the natives could see them. Whenever a native
espied the carcasses, he at once covered his face
with his hands, so as not to perceive or smell
them.

On one of the islands, it was the custom of the
natives to worship the first thing they saw, when
they went out in the morning, as their god

throughout the day. It was on this island, called Gilolo, that Pigafetta found some bamboos growing near the shore, "as thick as a man's leg," which contained in their hollow interior a a kind of water, which he found very excellent to drink. The king of the island had no less than five hundred children.

The King of Tidor was much grieved when he found that Espinosa had begun to suspect his intentions; and came almost weeping to him, to assure him of his good faith. Taking a Koran, the king put it on his head four or five times, then kissed it, and swore by Mohamet to be true to the Spanish sovereign. Espinosa was now convinced that he had wronged the king; the more so, when soon after he learned that some of the native chiefs had tried to persuade the king to kill all the Spaniards, but that he had sternly resisted their demand.

At last the time came to take leave of the Moluccas, and to set out on the voyage homeward. But just as the final preparations for departure had been made, and the ships had actually started, a serious accident happened. The " Victoria" sailed first; the " Trinidad" was about to follow, when one of the sailors discovered that she was leaking very badly in the hold. In all haste some of the men discharged her cargo, piling it on the strand, at hap-hazard ; while others worked with desperate energy at the pumps. This con- tinued all day ; but the labor was a vain one. The water spurted into the ship as if forced in by a large pump ; and it continually gained in the hold.

On hearing of this serious mishap, the king of Tidor at once offered the Admiral his aid. He brought with him five or six native divers, who, putting on large masks, plunged under the waves, and searched for some time for the place where the ship leaked. The divers went under with their hair all loose, thinking that their long locks, when they came near the leak, would be sucked to- wards it, and thus show where it was. But noth- ing could be discovered, and Espinosa was forced to abandon all hope of making his good flag-ship seaworthy again.

It only remained to transfer so much of his cargo to the " Victoria " as the latter would safely hold, and leave the " Trinidad " behind. The king said that he had more than two hundred carpen-

ters, and that they should be set to work repair-
ing the ship; and that if her crew would remain at
Tidor till she was whole, they should be cared
for "as if they were his own children." These
generous offers touched Espinosa's heart, and he
finally decided to accept them. The east winds,
favorable to a westward voyage, were now steadily
blowing; and it was full time for the "Victoria"
to take advantage of them and be off. At the
last moment, Espinosa resolved to remain at
Tidor, and to share the fate of the faithful crew
of the ship he had so long commanded. With
him staid fifty-three men. Meanwhile he confided the command of the returning "Victoria" to
his brave lieutenant, Juan Elcano, who, with a
crew of forty-seven Europeans, and thirteen
Malay prisoners who had been captured in the
boats, at once made ready to set sail for the
Cape of Good Hope.

On Saturday, the 21st of December, 1520, the
king of Tidor visited the Spaniards for the last
time. He brought on board the "Victoria" two
Malay pilots, whom he offered to Elcano to conduct the ship safely beyond the islands, and into
the Indian Ocean. He embraced the captain,

with many protestations of friendship; and as he
bade adieu to him, he shed many tears.

The "Victoria" set sail about mid-day. Espinosa and his companions, who were to remain
until the "Trinidad" was repaired, and was ready
to follow her sister-ship, accompanied the "Victoria" some distance beyond the bay, in their
long-boats. The king also, with several barges,
proceeded for many miles side by side with the
departing ship. As the "Victoria" finally emerged
from the bay where she had met with a hospitality so bounteous and evidently sincere, her
guns boomed a parting salute to the dis-
abled "Trinidad," and from the decks of the
latter an echoing "God-speed" was given by the
mouths of the cannon to the vessel homeward-
bound.

The "Victoria," guided by the faithful pilots
provided by the king of Tidor, sailed southwestward from that island, and soon the Moluccas
were lost to view. The voyagers were still, however, in the midst of the Archipelago, with its
innumerable shoals of isles; and day after day
they progressed across a sea teeming with beauti-
fully green and fertile spots, and among oriental

races strangely differing from each other in features and customs.

Elcano was eager to get back to Spain, and to at last accomplish the tour of the whole world. On the other hand, he desired to carry back to his sovereign as complete an account of the Archipelago as possible. As he sailed in the direction of the Indian Ocean, therefore, he made it a point to stop here and there at the islands, where it was evident that he would meet with a friendly reception, and to observe their people and productions.

He was continually surprised by the natural richness and beauty of the islands he passed, and in the bays of which he anchored. Everywhere there was the greatest abundance of tropical fruits, and especially of spices. He found that the inhabitants of many of these islands were cannibals, who did not hesitate to feast on the prisoners they captured in their numerous wars; others were Mohammedans, and betrayed many indications of being quite civilized and intelligent. On one island, he found the coast peopled by one race, followers of the Prophet, and the interior by a totally different race, who were ferocious, savage, and inveterate man-eaters.

While the "Victoria" was proceeding south-ward, she encountered, between Buru and Solor, two of the larger islands, one of those sudden, tremendous tornadoes, or wind storms, which often burst unexpectedly, almost out of a clear sky, in the tropics. For two days destruction seemed inevitable. At one moment the good ship was on the very point of dashing her ribs to splinters on the rocks of an island; at another, she threatened to founder in a terrific whirlpool. There were times when the desperate crew were all ready to give up, and cease longer to resist the overpowering fury of the elements. But Elcano refused to give way to despair. He shared the labors of his men, and by his example made them ashamed of their faltering; and as soon as the tempest subsided a little, he succeeded in bringing the "Victoria" into the shelter of an island bay.

Landing on the beach, the Spaniards soon found themselves surrounded by the fiercest and most savage-looking people they had yet seen. One of the strangest things was, that while the men stood aloof, in staring groups, the women advanced boldly and threateningly towards the strangers, and drew their bows, as if about to shoot a volley of arrows among them. Elcano sent one of his Malay pilots to them with some presents, however, and soon succeeded in pacify-ing them.

These people wore their shaggy hair in a very peculiar fashion. The thick and tangled locks were raised high above the head, held there by long combs made of cane; somewhat after the manner of the grand ladies of France and Eng-land a century ago. The men, moreover, wrapped their beards up in leaves in a very curious way, or enclosed them in the tubes of reeds. They went almost entirely naked; and Elcano shud-dered when some of the chiefs, thinking to per-form an act of hospitality, invited him and his companions to a feast composed of some of their dead enemies.

The "Victoria" remained a fortnight at this island, which was called Mallua, during which time her sides, worn by the storm, were carefully caulked. Meanwhile her cargo was increased by the wax, pepper, cocoanuts, and fowl which the island produced in great abundance.

She next passed a little island, the people of
which were of such low stature that the Spaniards
were fain to call them dwarfs. They had, moreover, very long ears: their voices were very shrill
and squeaky; they shaved their faces closely,
and had their dwellings underground, in rude
caves. Their only food was fish, and the pith of
a certain tree.

A few days after, the provisions of the ship
having become well-nigh exhausted, and the
natives of the islands in that vicinity not prov-
ing friendly, Elcano resolved to obtain supplies
by a trick. A few Spaniards landed on the
shore of a large island called Timor, and sent
word to the chief of the nearest village that
they wished to speak with him. He came to
them very timidly; but on their attempting to
make a bargain with him for some pigs and goats,
he became bolder, and demanded a high price for
them. Whereupon the Spaniards seized him,
hurried him into their boat, and rowed away
with him to the ship. They threatened him
with death unless he would send to his village an
order to return some pigs and goats, as his ran-
som. The poor chief was frightened almost out

of his wits, and made all haste to obey his captors. In due time the pigs and goats arrived, and the chief was sent home rejoicing, with some cloths, hatchets, scissors, and looking-glasses which Elcano thought it right to give him.

The voyagers had now reached the eastern end of that extensive series of islands, lying almost in a straight line from east to west, which ends in the long island of Java, and northwest of Java, Sumatra. But now the "Victoria" was supplied with as many provisions as she could hold; though worn with so long a voyage, she was still weather-tight and water-tight; and there seemed no reason to land at any more of the islands in the Archipelago.

Elcano therefore kept his course southward of Java, the long line of its hilly coast appearing dimly for many days on the north of him. He skirted also the coast of Sumatra, and at last found himself fairly launched on the Indian Ocean. He then kept his direction southwesterly, passing many leagues to the southward of Ceylon, and made as straight a course as possible to the

Cape of Good Hope. It was December when
he left Timor, his last stopping-place in the
Eastern seas; his eyes did not greet the
Cape of Good Hope until late in the following
May.

CHAPTER XVIII.

THE "VICTORIA" REACHES SPAIN.

HE voyage of the "Victoria" across the vast Indian Ocean, though long, was a prosperous one. The trade-winds blew from the east, nor did many perilous storms compel the crew to desperate exertion. No stirring incident attended their passage. One day was like the rest ; stiff breezes swelled the sails ; the sun shone, most often, bright over-head ; the waters, crested with foam by the winds, sparkled beneath its rays.

But on reaching the vicinity of the Cape of Good Hope, the wind suddenly changed. It now blew directly against them, and it was with difficulty that the "Victoria" could advance, even so slowly, along the African coast that was now constantly in sight.

Happily, Elcano had now reached a region

which had become well known. His charts, and
the records of previous voyagers, told him very
nearly where he was, and what course it was
wisest to take to reach his destination. He was
now, indeed, in the very track which, nearly a
quarter of a century before, Vasco da Gama had
traversed for the first time in his memorable voyage to India.

So unfavorable had now become the weather,
that the sailors began to clamor to put in at
some African port; and when they came opposite the large town of Mozambique, which they
knew to have been settled by the Portuguese,
their demands to seek shelter in its harbor became very eager. But Elcano had a good reason
for resisting the importunities of his men. Magellan's expedition had been undertaken against
the bitter opposition of the Portuguese; one of
its objects was to secure for Spain the allegiance
of the Moluccas, which the Portuguese claimed
as a part of the world which had been conceded
to them as a consequence of their discoveries. If
he should put in at a Portuguese station, he
might reasonably expect that he and his crew
would be taken prisoners, and the " Victoria'

seized and confiscated. He resolved, therefore, to push steadily on to the Cape.

The trials and hardships of the crew were now very serious. The good ship, after so much voyaging, had again become leaky, and the men with difficulty kept her from filling, by constant work at the pumps. Their provisions were low, and they were reduced to small daily rations of rice and water; their meat having decayed for want of salt. Many of the men, moreover, fell sick, and some died. At last the Cape came in sight; but it was dangerous to attempt to round it. For some weeks the "Victoria" was tossed about off the coast, vainly seeking a favorable opportunity to double the cape. They were finally forced to make a circuit, at a distance of fifteen miles from the headlands, in order to reach the western shore of the continent.

The ship's course was thence northwestward. Elcano determined to keep at sea, at least until the Cape Verde Islands were reached; and the voyage from the Cape to these islands lasted about two months. The weather was again propitious; but the sickness on board increased, and before the "Victoria" came in sight of the Cape Verdes, twenty-one men had perished.

One day the Cape Verdes appeared, dotting the summer sea in the distant horizon. Elcano for a while hesitated whether he should touch at them or not. They were possessions, like Mozambique, of the Portuguese. Would it be safe to trust himself in their hands? The misery of his crew, however, their sickness and want of food, finally decided him to run the risk.

As the "Victoria" approached Santiago, the southernmost of the group, it occurred to Elcano that he would tell the Portuguese that he had come from America, and that he had been driven out of his course by a terrible tempest. They would not then suspect that he had really been among the disputed islands of the East, but would be persuaded that he had sailed from Spanish settlements. This artful story at first had its intended effect. The "Victoria" entered the harbor, and was well received. Her sick were taken on shore and tended; and a boat-load of rice was sent on board. But soon it appeared that the Portuguese began to suspect the truth, that the "Victoria" had really come around the Cape. The second boat that went ashore was detained and the thirteen men in her were seized; at the same time, the Portuguese ships in the harbor were evidently being armed, with the purpose, no doubt, of capturing the " Victoria."

Elcano, who had been carefully on the watch, no sooner saw these signs of hostility, than, leaving the thirteen prisoners to their fate, he made haste to sail away. The voyage to Spain was now happily a short and comparatively easy one. He succeeded in escaping from the Portuguese ships, which, when they saw him departing, followed him for some leagues.

It was on the 6th day of September, 1522, a few days less than three years after she had set out, with her sister-ships, on her memorable voyage, that the weather-beaten "Victoria" came in sight of the familiar shores of Spain. The sailors—of whom there were only eighteen exhausted and half-famished men left of the gallant company that had set out—were full of joy at beholding their native land once more. They fired their cannon, and hung out their flags, and tearfully embraced each other; and as the ships drew nearer and nearer the port of San Lucar, the very port from which they had sailed, they eagerly pointed out the well-known landmarks to each other.

On entering the bay, they were greeted by the ships and boats anchored in it; and presently some of their countrymen came on board. When these learned that the vessel was the "Victoria," and that she had completed the circuit of the globe, they could scarcely believe their ears.

"Why," they exclaimed, "you were given up for lost, long, long ago! Surely, your return is a wonderful miracle!"

The news of the arrival of one of Magellan's ships was soon noised through the town, and was quickly carried up the river to Seville. The next day she was fairly surrounded by boats, and her deck was crowded with curious and de-lighted visitors. The governor of the district came on board, embraced Elcano, and gave orders that the sailors, who were half-dead from sickness, hunger, and their many hardships, should be taken on shore and tenderly cared for.

But no sooner had they set foot on land, than the poor fellows, staggering from weakness, formed into line, and walked as well as they could to a church; where, kneeling before the altar, they offered up a thanksgiving for their safe arrival home.   Then they allowed themselves to be carried to the houses of the people and treated to the best the town afforded.

The day following, the men returned to the "Victoria," and she sailed up the river to Seville, and cast anchor near the mole, on the very spot whence she had set sail.   The old city was full of excitement and commotion at her arrival. Crowds thronged the quay, and the mayor and other dignitaries hastened to give public welcome to the heroic voyagers.

Once more the cannon of the " Victoria" awoke the echoes with their hoarse voices of joy.   The brave bunting was flung to the breeze, and gay garlands decked mast and gunwale.   Here, as at San Lucar, the wanderers' first thought was to render thanks to God for their preservation from countless perils.   The people of Seville, in dense masses along the pavements, and choking every window, saw the sunburnt mariners pass in procession, in their shirt-sleeves, bare-footed, and each bearing a taper, to the ancient and imposing church of Santa Maria del Antigua, where they attended mass, and joined with all their souls in the thanksgiving prayers offered up by the priests.

Thence they hastened to the public square, where, you may well believe, they were soon wrapt in the embraces of parents, wives, children, and friends. The tender-hearted Sevillians could not witness, without tearful emotion, the haggard and hungry features, the emaciated forms, and the tottering steps of the men who had gone out from their midst three years before, ruddy and stout and strong; nor was it less pitiful to see the anguish and hear the cries of the poor widows who sought in vain, in the little group, for husbands who had departed in the ships, but whom they would never look upon again.

Into the square came a lady, young and fair, leading a little girl two or three years old. She leaned on the arm of a grizzled, but still erect and haughty cavalier. She was attired in deep black, and there were traces of long mourning on her pale cheeks; and now, as she slowly approached the returned crew, she could not suppress her profound emotions.

As if by instinct, the sailors knew at once that she was the lady Beatrix, the widow of their beloved Admiral, whose brave soul had departed from earth in the far eastern seas; that the little girl was Magellan's daughter, whom he had never seen; and that the old cavalier who escorted Beatrix was her father, Don Diego Barbosa.

They had come, with sad but eager hearts, to welcome back the comrades of him they had never ceased to mourn since his heroic death in a distant land.

Throughout Spain, and, indeed, Europe, the news of the arrival of the "Victoria" and her successful voyage round the world, spread rapidly, and caused a great commotion. The king, who, soon after the departure of Magellan's expedition, had become emperor of Germany, and who, at twenty-two, had shown himself one of the ablest and most energetic monarchs in Christendom, no sooner heard that the "Victoria" was safe at Seville, than he dispatched a courier to that city, inviting Elcano and all his comrades to go and visit him at his court in Valladolid.

As soon as they could get ready, therefore, the voyagers proceeded to Valladolid, where the Emperor Charles received them with a splendid welcome, in the midst of his grandees and courtiers. Elcano told his sovereign the story of their adventures, to which Charles listened with breathless interest ; and when the tale was done, the emperor ordered apartments to be prepared for the sailors in the town, while he entertained the officers in the palace itself.

Not content with this hospitality, Charles gave a handsome pension to each of the survivors of this memorable expedition ; and granted to their gallant captain, Elcano, a coat-of-arms, which displayed on its shield some gold nutmegs and cloves, and an image of the globe, with the motto upon it, "You were the first to circumnavigate me."

One strange thing happened when the "Victoria" arrived at Seville, which at first puzzled Elcano very much. According to his reckonings, which he had carefully kept every day from the starting of the expedition, the date of his arrival was the 5th of September. But on talking with the people at Seville, he found that, with them, it was the 6th. During the voyage, therefore, he had lost a day. How could this have happened? He knew that he had kept his calendar correctly, and had never omitted to score each twenty-four hours; and yet, undoubtedly, it was the 6th, and not the 5th, on which he had reached Seville.

The emperor submitted this problem to a famous astronomer, Contarini; who, after studying it, discovered the clue.   He showed that the loss of a day was the natural result of the voyage from east to west, in which they kept company with the sun; and that, if they had gone the other way, from west to east, they would have gained a day.   This was one of the most valuable facts ascertained by Magellan's expedition.

The fate of the "Trinidad," which had been left behind at Tidor, remains to be told.   In due time, with the aid of the native carpenters, she was repaired and made ready to resume her voyage.   But Espinosa, fearing lest the Portuguese in India, who had now heard of the presence of the Spaniards in the Moluccas, should attack him, resolved to sail, not westward, in the track of the "Victoria," but eastward across the Pacific again, in the hope of reaching the Spanish settlement of Panama.

The voyage was a terrible one.   Furious storms constantly assailed the devoted ship; and after

being tossed many weeks amid them, the "Trinidad" was forced to return to the Moluccas. Unfortunately the Portuguese had now reached
those islands with a large force of men; and no
sooner had the storm-beaten "Trinidad" put into
port, than she was attacked and overwhelmed by
Portuguese vessels of war. Espinosa and all his
comrades were taken, and cast into prison. There
they were treated with such barbaric cruelty,
and were seized with such severe distempers,
that one after another died, including Espinosa
himself; until at last only four miserable crea-
tures, out of all that gallant crew, were left. The
Portuguese took pity on these, and shipped them
home, four years after the return of the "Victoria," in one of their own ships.

Thus was completed the famous expedition by
which the route to Asia around South America
was found; which first traversed the broad expanse of the Pacific, that received its name from
the intrepid commander; which made the first
tour of the entire globe, and brought to light the
fact of the loss of a day by sailing with the sun,
from east to west.

Its fame is most of all due to the heroic and

noble-hearted Fernan Magellan, who conceived the great idea which it fulfilled; who, in spite of enormous obstacles, and after having been rejected by his own country, succeeded in raising the fleet and obtaining its command; who conducted it through many perils over the greater part of its long course; and who, though he unhappily died too soon to reap the full reward of his achievements, at least left a name and fame imperishable in the annals of discovery.

HEROES OF HISTORY SERIES

A NEWLY grouped collection of standard favorites—the kind that never grow old. In school and public libraries and intelligent homes these books are recognized as outweighing any number of the trashy newer juveniles so much in evidence, and for bright boys and girls they hold a high interest. The pleasing new covers, at the same low price, give them a renewed welcome.

Twenty titles by unsurpassed writers of history for the young: Towle, Headley, Bogart, Watson, and Frost.

New cover design, with side titles. Illustrated. Price per volume, 60 cents.

By GEORGE M. TOWLE

1. DRAKE; The Sea King of Devon.
2. MAGELLAN; First Around the World.
3. MARCO POLO; His Travels and Adventures.
4. PIZARRO; His Adventures and Conquests.
5. RALEGH; His Voyages and Adventures.
6. VASCO DA GAMA; His Voyages and Adventures.
7. HEROES AND MARTYRS OF INVENTION.

By P. C. HEADLEY

8. FACING THE ENEMY; Life of Gen. W. T. Sherman.
9. FIGHT IT OUT ON THIS LINE; Life of Gen. U. S. Grant.

By W. H. BOGART

10. BORDER BOY; Life of Daniel Boone.

By HENRY C. WATSON

11. FATHER OF HIS COUNTRY; Life of Washington.
12. FRIEND OF WASHINGTON; Life of Lafayette.
13. GREAT PEACEMAKER; Life of William Penn.
14. POOR RICHARD'S STORY; Life of Franklin.

By JOHN FROST

15. GREAT EXPOUNDER; Life of Daniel Webster
16. LITTLE CORPORAL; Life of Napoleon.
17. OLD HICKORY; Life of Andrew Jackson.
18. OLD ROUGH AND READY; Life of Gen. Zachary Taylor.
19. MILL BOY OF THE SLASHES; Life of Henry Clay.
20. SWAMP FOX; Life of Gen. Francis Marion.

LOTHROP, LEE & SHEPARD CO., BOSTON

A Boy of a Thousand Years Ago

By HARRIET T. COMSTOCK 12mo

Profusely illustrated with full-page drawings and chapter headings by GEORGE VARIAN $1.00

IT will at once be understood that the "boy" of the story is Alfred the Great in his youth, but it cannot be understood how delightful a story this is until it is seen and read. The splendid pictures of George Varian make this book superior among juveniles.

"Not a boy lives who will not enjoy this book thoroughly. There is a good deal of first-class historical information woven into the story, but the best part of it is the splendid impression of times and manners it gives in old England a thousand years ago."—*Louisville Courier-Journal.*

"Mrs. Comstock writes very appreciatively of Little Alfred, who was afterward the Great, and from mighty meagre materials creates a story that hangs together well. The illustrations for this volume are especially beautiful."—*Boston Home Journal.*

The Story of Joan of Arc FOR BOYS AND GIRLS

By KATE E. CARPENTER Illustrated by AMY BROOKS, also from paintings, and with map Large 12mo Cloth $1.00

THE favorite story of Joan of Arc is here treated in a uniquely attractive way. "Aunt Kate" tells the story of Joan of Arc to Master Harold, aged 11, and to Misses Bessie and Marjorie, aged 10 and 8, respectively, to their intense delight. They look up places on the map, and have a fine time while hearing the thrilling story, told in such simple language that they can readily understand it all. Parents and teachers will also be greatly interested in this book from an educational point of view.

"The tale is well told and the children will delight in it."—*Chicago Post.*

"Told so simply and clearly that young readers cannot fail to be entertained and instructed."—*Congregationalist, Boston.*

For sale by all booksellers or sent postpaid on receipt of price by the publishers.

LOTHROP, LEE & SHEPARD CO., BOSTON

BRAVE HEART SERIES

By Adele E. Thompson

Illustrated   12mo   Cloth   *Net* $1.25 each

Betty Seldon, Patriot

A BOOK that is at the same time fascinating and noble. Historical events are accurately traced leading up to the surrender of Cornwallis at Yorktown, with reunion and happiness for all who deserve it

Brave Heart Elizabeth

IT is a story of the making of the Ohio frontier, much of it taken from life, and the heroine one of the famous Zane family after which Zanesville, O., takes its name. An accurate, pleasing, and yet at times intensely thrilling picture of the stirring period of border settlement.

A Lassie of the Isles

THIS is the romantic story of Flora Macdonald, the lassie of Skye, who aided in the escape of Charles Stuart, otherwise known as the "Young Pretender."

Polly of the Pines

THE events of the story occur in the years 1775-82. Polly was an orphan living with her mother's family, who were Scotch Highlanders, and for the most part intensely loyal to the Crown. Polly finds the glamor of royal adherence hard to resist, but her heart turns towards the patriots and she does much to aid and encourage them.

American Patty

A Story of 1812

PATTY is a brave, winsome girl of sixteen whose family have settled across the Canadian border and are living in peace and prosperity, and on the best of terms with the neighbors and friendly Indians. All this is suddenly and entirely changed by the breaking out of war, and unwillingness on the part of her father and brother to serve against their native land brings distress and deadly peril.

For sale by all booksellers, or sent postpaid on receipt of price by the publishers

LOTHROP, LEE & SHEPARD CO., BOSTON

Famous Children

By H. Twitchell   Illustrated $1.25 *net*

WE have here a most valuable book, telling not of the childhood of those who have afterwards become famous, but those who as children are famous in history, song, and story. For convenience the subjects are grouped as " Royal Children," " Child Artists," " Learned Children," " Devoted Children," " Child Martyrs," and " Heroic Children," and the names of the " two little princes," Louis XVII., Mozart, St. Genevieve, David, and Joan of Arc are here, as well as those of many more.

The Story of the Cid   For Young People

By Calvin Dill Wilson   Illustrated by J. W. Kennedy $1.25 *net*

MR. WILSON, a well-known writer and reviewer, has prepared from Southey's translation, which was far too cumbrous to entertain the young, a book that will kindle the imagination of youth and entertain and inform those of advanced years.

Jason's Quest

By D. O. S. Lowell, A. M., M. D.   Illustrated $1.00 *net*

NOTHING can be better to arouse the imagination of boys and girls, and at the same time store in their minds knowledge indispensable to any one who would be known as cultured, or happier than Professor Lowell's way of telling a story, and the many excellent drawings have lent great spirit to the narrative.

Heroes of the Crusades

By Amanda M. Douglas   Cloth   Fifty illustrations $1.35 *net*

THE romantic interest in the days of chivalry, so fully exemplified by the " Heroes of the Crusades," is permanent and properly so.   This book is fitted to keep it alive without descending to improbability or cheap sensationalism.

For sale by all booksellers or sent postpaid on receipt of price by the publishers,

LOTHROP, LEE & SHEPARD CO., BOSTON

New Editions of Two Favorite Books

THE LANCE OF KANANA
A STORY OF ARABIA

By HARRY W. FRENCH ("Abd el Ardavan")
Two-color illustrations by Garrett   Net, $1.00

KANANA, a Bedouin youth, though excelling in athletic prowess, is branded, even by his father, as a coward because he prefers the humble lot of a shepherd to the warrior's career that he, the son of a sheik known as the "Terror of the Desert," was expected to follow. "Only for Allah and Arabia will I lift a lance and take a life," he maintained. Opportunity to prove his worth soon comes, and the supposed coward, understood too late, becomes in memory a national hero.

"The stirring story of the loyalty and self-sacrifice of a Bedouin boy is well worth the attractive new edition in which it now presents its rare picture of fervid patriotism."—*Continent, Chicago.*

THE ADVENTURES
OF MILTIADES PETERKIN PAUL

By JOHN BROWNJOHN

Frontispiece by John Goss   Illustrated by "Boz"
Quarto   Net, $1.00

HERE is a child classic reissued in a finer and handsomer form, in response to the persistent demand of those who know the mirth-provoking quality of the exploits of the ingenious small boy named Miltiades Peterkin Paul and spoken of as "a great traveler, although he was small." Whoever has once enjoyed the story of the restless little lad who imitated Don Quixote, and did many other things, is permanently charmed by it.

"This youthful Don Quixote, with his travels and exploits, drives 'dull care' away from the elders and delights the juniors."—*Watchman, N. Y.*